Amos 3:3

Can two walk together, except they be agreed?

OTHER BOOKS:

THE POWER
OF THE
ANOINTING

BRUCE HINES

CONTENTS

FOREWORD

When I met Bruce in 2002 he had already been walking with the Lord for 8 years. When we started dating, everywhere we went the anointing on both of our lives produced what is called today, Power Evangelism. Now that we are married and our walk with God has become even more intimate our entire lives are consumed with a drive to demonstrate the Love of God. Admittedly, the anointing on Bruce's life is much greater than mine. Like I said before, he is 8 years ahead of me! But after reading this book I'm even more determined to chase the Lord, expecting an increase of the Lords anointing on my life.

I've watched Bruce's love for the Lord grow, causing a progression of fruit to increase over the years. I've be there when he started ministering in the private ministry rooms and watched the slow progression to minister corporately. I've observed the Lord increase the anointing on Bruce's life as he was sent to minister in the streets, in drug rehabilitation centers and into churches. The Lord moved powerfully in every situation with deliverance, inner healing, physical healing and miracles. I have seen the Lord use my husband is too many ways to document.

> *There are many more things that Jesus did. If all of them were written down, I suppose that not even the world itself would have space for the books that would be written. John 21:25*

I'm excited for you to read through the pages of this book. You're going to be amazed at all the knowledge the Lord has revealed to Bruce about how to be in a relationship with God. Wait until you see his passion for the Lord poured out on these pages. It will inspire a great measure of Love in your heart to have the Lord be your best friend. At the end of this book you will have a drive to be closer with the Father, the Son and the Holy Spirit. Out of that relationship you will see an increase in the anointing on your life. Before you know it, God will be encountering people through YOU, in greater measures than He already is.

With expectations for your journey with the Lord,

Leah Hines
Co-Founder and Co-Pastor
Church in One Accord
www.churchinoneaccord.org

INTRODUCTION

In the creation's beginning account, God placed Adam in the garden to enjoy not only a friendship with God, but to commune with Him. Communion with God is to live in harmony, spirit, soul, and body so that a closeness through God's presence, a man may communicate with God. I could even say, man becomes a friend of God. As we will learn, communion is to come into a common faith with God. The believer is to experience God in all His attributes. We are to share in God's expressions toward us and to become a family member of God the Father, God the Son, and God the Holy Spirit. Fellowship is a powerful word in the Bible! It speaks of companionship or togetherness, an association or alliance who share in the same interests. We could say, the Bible calls fellowship a walking with God. For the anointing to be activated and powerfully beneficial, the believer must walk in fellowship with God.

Every believer must have the anointing of the Holy Spirit! The baptism of the Holy Spirit is for us personally, but the anointing is if I may, the baptism on steroids. It is from the anointing that the work of God flows, that is, the acceptable work of God. The Holy Spirit's anointing is not a mystery or something that has been hidden, but was demonstrated by the Trinity. In Acts 10:38, God the Father anointed God the Son with God the Holy Spirit and power. The result of being anointed is power! Habakkuk 3:4 says, His brightness was like the light; He had rays flashing from His hand, And there His power was hidden.

What Habakkuk is saying, God's anointing (His power) hides in His presence; so there is power in His presence. Every time God's presence comes, the measure of the presence reveals the measure of the power! The King James Bible uses horns instead of rays, but both mean strength and power of a king. The figurative meaning is granting victory or bestowing prosperity.

Amos says, "Can two walk together, unless they are agreed?" We see in the form of a question, agreement is the solution to walking together. Amos is telling us that if we are to walk with God, we must be united and a likeness. Yes, we are to take on the likeness of the Lord Jesus Christ. This is the definition of together! We are to be joined for a common purpose and we are to have common feelings.

The anointing is God's power and is the manifestation and the result of His presence. As I have said before, there is no substitute for the anointing of God. It is the oil of heaven that empowers the believer to walk with Christ in extreme levels. From the beginning God has revealed to mankind that His priority has been fellowship. This is clearly demonstrated today in what the Church calls soaking. The anointing is God's power, but the presence is His person. So we must have the presence so that the anointing will work properly. Priority is a fact or condition of being what is regarded and treated as of most importance. Is this how most believers examine the Word of God? We all want to be anointed, but we value our beliefs, thoughts and ways over transforming to God's. We must be able to see God's priorities if we expect the anointing to expand our capacity. Without an increase in the believer's life, that one becomes stagnate and no longer pliable. When this takes place, the believers position in the spirit world diminishes and the anointing seems not to be as effective.

In our growth and our walking with God, experiencing the power of the anointing, we must focus on what God is doing now in our lives. We will not move on to the next phrase or season in our life until God has established excellence in the season we are in. This is a reality that very few believers pay attention too. The believer wants more from God, yet they do not establish God's excellence in themselves for the season they are in. So, if you are a servant of God, understand this, there will be no new season until God is satisfied by creating His excellence in our life. This is what Paul is alluding too, an eternal excellence that far out weights the things of the temporal. Yes, God wants the eternal to manifest over the temporal. This excellence and moral goodness stands the test of eternity; something that will not fade or wither; something that will pass through the fire and have an eternal weight in eternity.

We now realize that whatever happens in time is of secondary importance in shaping our eternal character; for what we are in our character is eternal.

We must understand the season we are in and what we must learn in that season. There will be a presence for that season to encourage us, to make us established in the realities of that season. Always remember that in all things, nothing is to go to waste. Every success and every failure is the hand of God. Each through the process educating us in the supernatural and the Kingdom of Heaven. So every season will start with a seed principle. Think about what I am saying; develop patience and endurance, these are key in the anointing's growth. Like anything with God, both the presence and the anointing will grow as we walk with God.

Bruce Hines

Author and Sr. Pastor
Church in One Accord

CHAPTER ONE

AN INVITATION TO WALK WITH GOD

As I open this powerful revelation of walking with God, I expect that the reader will accept the challenge and feel the urgent call as I do through the writing of this book, a calling to walk with God on a deeper level.

The New Testament in its essence is an invitation to share fellowship with God and the Apostles. From the beginning, the essence of the Christian life is to have fellowship with God. What the Apostle John states is that the born-again believer is to have an intrinsic nature so deeply rooted that fellowship with God becomes natural. This is stated so clearly and in such a way as to allow an accurate perception and interpretation without doubt by John. John wants us to understand and comprehend this deep and personal, intimate relationship believers are called too.

That which was from the beginning, which we have heard, which we have seen with our eyes, which we have looked upon, and our hands have handled, concerning the Word of life— the life was manifested, and we have seen, and bear witness, and declare to you that eternal life which was with the Father and was manifested to us—that which we have seen and heard we declare to you, that you also may have fellowship with us; and truly our fellowship is with the Father and with His Son Jesus Christ. And these things we write to you that your joy may be full. 1 John 1:1-4 NKJV

In the creation's beginning account, God placed Adam in the garden to enjoy not only a friendship with God, but to commune with Him. Communion with God is to live in harmony, spirit, soul, and body so that a closeness through God's presence, a man may communicate with God. I could even say, man becomes a friend of God. As we learn from first John, communion is to come into a common faith with God. The believer is to experience God in all His attributes. We are to share in God's expressions toward us and to become a family member of God the Father, God the Son, and God the Holy Spirit. This intimate relationship described by the Apostle John, in which we have heard, which we have seen with our eyes, which we have looked upon, and our hands have handled, concerning the Word of life is an intimate account. John is stating that the Apostles relationship with Jesus was as the beginning, like God and Adam. He also shows we too can have this fellowship.

John describes a beginning with mankind that would be a foundation and a sphere of influence in God. The Church calls this sphere, God's presence with intimacy. The Holy Spirit instantly desires to transform the believer through His presence and the Word of God as we walk in agreement.

John gives the reason the New Testament was passed on to us by the Apostles. He says the ultimate purpose in verse three is that you also may have fellowship with us; and truly our fellowship is with the Father and with His Son Jesus Christ. Today, this fellowship is through the presence and power of the Holy Spirit. It would be good to point out that this sphere of influence is immeasurable. Mankind has been designed today through the Holy Spirit to meet Him, the Holy Spirit personally and intimately. When this happens to the believer that one is transformed drastically into another person. So let me say it this way, the New Testament is a written document from God through the hands of the Apostles to come into and enjoy the fellowship that God the Father and God the Son have together eternally.

As we invite the Holy Spirit to transform us, we start a journey of personal friendship. He is to be our continual guide, leading us into righteousness and holiness. This sanctification process comes from a deep desire to have intimacy and fellowship with God's Spirit. The day I was touched by the Holy Spirit, I was driven by God's Spirit

And nature to spend time in His presence and His Word. Little did I know God's Spirit was leading me so that the operation of the anointing would begin. So let us not miss the purpose for why the New Testament was given to the Church, and that is fellowship with God.

Before moving on, there is one more motive for John's writing. In verse four, these things we write to you that your joy may be full. Joy is not only a fruit of the Holy Spirit but an attribute. So many don't understand holy laughter as labeled today. Joy results from entering into fellowship with God as that joy is to be a fulness of joy, in other words, beyond containment.

Walking With God

Fellowship is a powerful word in the Bible! It speaks of companionship or togetherness, an association or alliance who share in the same interests. We could say, the Bible calls fellowship a walking with God. When a husband and wife go on a walk together, they are having fellowship together. For the anointing to be activated and powerfully beneficial, the believer must walk in fellowship with God. We must come to understand and appreciate the power of unity when walking together. Walking is a journey! It is living in harmony with God. From harmony, comes the desire to abide in unity with God, this is when the anointing is powerful. The believer who learns to walk with God stays in step with God and we harmonize our thoughts so that it deepens our fellowship with God.

God desires us to walk with Him, He wants us to live in harmony with Him, and He wants our fellowship to be deepened. Micah reveals some basic requirements for the one who is to walk with God,

> *He has shown you, O man, what is good;*
> *And what does the Lord require of you*
> *But to do justly,*
> *To love mercy,*
> *And to walk humbly with your God?*
> *Micah 6:8 NKJV*

When we look at the Hebrew word humble, it literally means to humble one's self to walk with God. So what are God's three requirements stated there, to do justly (justice/righteousness), second, mercy and third, humility. Micah lists three aspects of character required to walk with God in fellowship so that the anointing can grow to the fullest. John states in 1 John that God is Light. The meaning is that He is holy and God's message is truthful, because He is perfect in righteousness. The Apostle John says if we say we have fellowship with God and yet walk in darkness of sin, we are not practicing or walking in the truth or fellowship. The Apostle connects fellowship as walking. What is scripture telling us? If we are too [really] walk with God and operate in the anointing, we must practice each day in conforming to the precepts of God's Word. The suggestion that John is making, if we walk in the Light, God's ways, we will have true unbroken fellowship with Him and He with us. This is the power of the anointing. We must do and desire what He is desiring and wanting to do.

Most charismatic believers want the anointing but are too selfish in heart to be anointed. Micah gives a list of requirements. The primary sense of šāpaṭ or justly is to exercise the processes of government. Justice is to decide a question of a legal right or wrong and thus determine the innocence or guilt of the accused and assign appropriate punishment or retribution. Most people don't understand this part of the anointing.

In today's Church, we want the blessings through the anointing but are unwilling to face our guilt and wrongdoing. The minute God's anointed man or woman prophesy judgment or said God will not heal or deliver you because of guilt, we would say that person was not acting in the character of love. Yet, this has happened as I have ministered! A woman was manifesting demons as I preached the gospel, but when I got her in a private ministry session to deal with the demons, nothing happened. I said, Lord, what is going on here. God said, she is not a tither! The minute she tithed the demons left her. The anointing is to exercise a series of actions or steps to achieve God's desired government. God's desire is to heal and deliver. He wants to assign punishment and inflict vengeance on the kingdom of darkness for their crimes. God's government is over all and He restricts evil by His rules or laws. Think about what I said before rejecting it. God blesses through love, yet He punishes for loves sake. God's anointing is to exercise God's government.

When Micah speaks of mercy or kindness, the sense is a kind act. The definition is loyalty or a joint obligation of faithfulness, goodness, and graciousness. We would know kindness or mercy in the New Testament as grace. When we are walking with God in mercy, we are taking part in an activity of the anointing that comes from His nature. Grace or mercy expresses the divine personality rather than as a lack of the movement of God's nature. What I am saying is this, it is a dimension of divine activity that enables God to deal with human rebellion in all its forms with an inexhaustible capacity to forgive and bless. God forgives but holds mankind accountable to bless. The anointing is to bring mercy and kindness to bless and to call people to repentance. The anointing then is an empowerment to bless and a weapon to break curse. The blessings of God cannot come unless mankind meets God's conditions.

Then Micah turns to the inward self of the one desiring to walk with God through the anointing. Humility is the opposite of pride, the nature man received through the fall. Humility goes to the root of the inner man to deal with pride. Humility is to submit to authority in a manner respectfully and is careful in direction, implying wise behavior. So we can conclude, wisdom is to the one who walks with God and power is given through the anointing. Humility is to humble one's self and to display wisdom!

ENOCH WALKS WITH GOD

In Hebrews 11:5 the Bible says by faith Enoch pleased God in such a way he was taken to heaven so he would not have a glimpse of death; Enoch could not be found because

God had taken him. Enoch's testimony was that he walked with God in such fellowship and harmony it pleased God to take him. Through the presence and anointing of God, Enoch became accustom to God's realm, and he was taken to heaven. This is the power of agreement! We are to agree with God's government that two realms collide through fellowship and harmony.

Genesis 5:21-24, Enoch walked in habitual fellowship, doing constantly what God desired and wanted, that God took him away to be at home with Him. Enoch could find the glory of God's presence and become one with God. In other words, Enoch became so much like God that he belonged more to God's realm, not this evil fallen age. What Enoch reveals is that the anointing is the consequence or manifestation of God's presence and glory and this is walking with God. The outstanding fact about Enoch according to scripture is he lived a life walking with God.

How did Enoch please God, by walking with God. How did he walk with God, by faith! We see God's purpose and invitation to share fellowship with Him by walking with Him. This is the ultimate secret to the anointing. Yes we need the presence and glory of God, but unless I am willing to walk with God in fellowship and exercise His government rule over the earth, the anointing will not do what it is meant too.

CHAPTER ONE

COMMISSIONED BY GOD

Jesus came up and said to them, "All authority
(all power of absolute rule) in heaven and on
earth has been given to Me. Go therefore and
make disciples of all the nations [help the people to
learn of Me, believe in Me, and obey My words],
baptizing them in the name of the Father and
of the Son and of the Holy Spirit, teaching them
to observe everything that I have commanded
you; and lo, I am with you always [remaining
with you perpetually—regardless of circum-
stance, and on every occasion], even to the end of
the age." Matthew 28:18-20 Amplified Bible

The great commission is the Church's orders from Jesus to exercise His rule within this fallen evil age. Very few
people understand the price that has to be paid within the
great commission. The commission is an official charge
with a particular function. It is instruction through command for a duty given through a superior. I could say a
commission is an order for work with authority given to
perform a task. It is an order that authorizes a person or
assembly to bring to readiness for active service.

God gives the anointing to fulfill the great commission!
The anointing is not without a price and heartache. Those
believers who seek to walk in fellowship with God, seek to
establish God's government on earth through the anointing, will be rejected by this world. Unbelievers or believers
who reject the anointing are rejecting God's government

and are under the control of a fallen angel over their life.

Jesus says in Matthew 22:14, For many are called, but few are chosen. Again, very few will pay the price to walk with God and go through the rejection of mankind. Remember how Enoch pleased God through faith? God will call you through His presence and watch to see how faithful you are to walk with Him. If the believer will give their heart for service, then the anointing will come. When we are chosen, God Himself will guard the anointing on our lives and seek to increase the authority and power of the anointing. The believer can be discharged from service through selfish desires and wants that seek to establish our own kingdom. People are let go from the anointing because they fail in one department, total death to self! I see this every Sunday when believers leave the sanctuary and go home without service. They chose not to clean up, minister healing and deliverance to the people or visit with the visitor! In Matthew 23:11-12, The greatest among you will be your servant. For those who exalt themselves will be humbled, and those who humble themselves will be exalted. Everyone who walks out the door without serving is exalting themselves.

Many will seek the call and desire the anointing, but when God sends a series of tests, most will be disqualified. Most will not trust God and walk with Him, leaving everything to the Lord to fulfill.

My son, give me your heart, And let your eyes
observe my ways. Proverbs 23:26 NKJV

We begin our service to the Lord by giving Him our hearts. This is walking with God! We give Him our mind, will, and emotions. We seek inner healing and deliverance to purify our lives. To observe God's ways is to say, I am through with my old life and the great commission is now my business.

WALKING IN AGREEMENT

Can two walk together, unless they are agreed? Amos 3:3 NKJV

As I have been guiding our thoughts in this first chapter, we are to express through thoughts and feeling a fellowship with God by walking with Him. I've been stating that the basic requirement of the believer who desires the anointing must agree with God. The Bible is so transparent on this subject and leaves no room for doubt or confusion. Look at the question in Amos, to agree means to harmonize in our ways and thoughts with God. The anointing is given for God's agenda, to establish the Kingdom of God in this fallen evil age.

It is impossible to walk with God and operate in the anointing unless we learn to harmonize with God in thoughts and actions. However, the scripture makes it clear by nature God's ways and thoughts are extremely different from ours.

This is stated with great clarity and transparency in Isaiah 55:6-9,

> *Seek the Lord while He may be found,*
> *Call upon Him while He is near.*
> *Let the wicked forsake his way,*
> *And the unrighteous man his thoughts;*
> *Let him return to the Lord,*
> *And He will have mercy on him;*
> *And to our God,*
> *For He will abundantly pardon.*
> *"For My thoughts are not your thoughts,*
> *Nor are your ways My ways," says the Lord.*
> *"For as the heavens are higher than the earth,*
> *So are My ways higher than your ways,*
> *And My thoughts than your thoughts.*

Isaiah is saying, it is not enough to turn to the Lord in an outward act or by going to Church. The inclusion of the qualifying element is while He may be found or while He is near. Everyone who hungers and thirsts for righteousness receives the invitation to walk with God. This is the outcome of forsaking inward thoughts and desires. Isaiah says, we are to come back so that God can have mercy on us. It is the believer who is willing to allow God to draw them to intimacy who is the one God will walk with.

Notice the reason God says, My thoughts are not your thoughts, nor your ways My ways. God is asking us to realize something of vital importance, His thoughts and ways! God implies that man's natural ways and thoughts are not in harmony with His. Then God through Isaiah gives us an example of an immeasurable gap as the heavens are higher than the earth. What an example! The more we are transformed into the image of Christ Jesus, the more we think and act like Him and the anointing grows.

> *Therefore, since Christ has suffered in the flesh, arm yourselves also with the same purpose, because he who has suffered in the flesh has ceased from sin, 2 so as to live the rest of the time in the flesh no longer for the lusts of men, but for the will of God. 1 Peter 4:1-2 NASB*

Peter wrote a great deal about the way believers' lives should differ from the ordinary pattern of the world. Peter states that the believer will suffer in the flesh (old man) until he puts an end to that state or activity. What I mean by state is the old man or carnal nature. Remember Isaiah said the old self or man does not think or desire what God wants. Until we put out of our lives the desires of the world, the anointing that comes through walking with God will not be effective. We feel the anointing desiring to operate, but because our thoughts and desires have not been surrendered unto death, the success in producing a desired or intended result through the anointing evades us.

Peter reminds us that Christ had suffered and died for sins, once for all, and that believers should be ready to suffer like the master. Peter says in 1 Peter 3:17, if we are to suffer, it should be for doing good, not for doing evil, in order to be a good witness to unbelievers. We must die to self and live to God, this is walking with God in harmony and the anointing. Are we ready to suffer for the anointing as Christ suffered? A good witness is the one who can reveal Jesus and His power. We have the message and the power to do the things Christ has called us too.

We are to arm ourselves, that is a military term. With what are we to arm ourselves? With the same attitude, thoughts, and ways that Christ had. This is where the anointing lives and breathes. It is like a breath of fresh air to the soul operating in the anointing and to the one that needs Christ Jesus' touch.

There is one more simple and obvious fact that we must discuss from Malachi 3:6,

> *"For I, the Lord, do not change; therefore*
> *you, O sons of Jacob, are not consumed."*

We should be thankful that God does not change. He doesn't change because He is perfect. God is declaring that, though He must punish Israel, yet He will not utterly destroy them, because He is unchanging in His covenant promises. So any change that is done, is on our part, not His. God will not change or adjust His ways and thoughts, we must!

Many believers claim that they are anointed, yet God states He works with what He can. It is so sad to see people waste away the anointing believing they are in the will of God. If we are to agree with God, we are to walk in His ways, agree with His thoughts or the Word of God, then and only then will the anointing flow all the time. How can two walk together unless they agree?

In recapping and concluding this chapter, I pointed out certain scriptural fundamental truths that relate to the anointing and walking or agreeing with God. The New Testament extends to us a call to share fellowship with God. This fellowship is pointed out frequently in the Bible as walking with God. To walk with God, we must agree with God. To agree is to harmonize in ways and thoughts. Through these steps, the anointing becomes effective. However, scripture teaches that by nature our ways and thoughts are not like God's ways and thoughts. Last, God does not change! This is the power of the anointing!

Chapter Two

Provision To Walk With God

What I love about the Bible is it shows us the things that are wrong and teaches us how to put things right. The Bibles ultimate push or effort is always positive. When the Bible reveals the negative, it is a message to us for our need of the positive. Let us examine a passage in scripture from a chapter in Isaiah 55:6-9,

Seek the Lord while He may be found,
Call upon Him while He is near.
Let the wicked forsake his way,
And the unrighteous man his thoughts;
Let him return to the Lord,
And He will have mercy on him;
And to our God,

For He will abundantly pardon.
"For My thoughts are not your thoughts,
Nor are your ways My ways," says the Lord.
"For as the heavens are higher than the earth,
So are My ways higher than your ways,
And My thoughts than your thoughts.

Isaiah says it is not just our outward actions, but our inward ways and thoughts. So the question we need to resolve is how do we bridge the immeasurable gap between God and man? One thing must be mentioned, man does not have the solution, it is God who must provide the answer.

"For as the rain and the snow come down from
heaven, and do not return there without watering
the earth and making it bear and sprout,
And furnishing seed to the sower and bread to the
eater; so will My word be which goes forth from My
mouth; it will not return to Me empty,
Without accomplishing what I desire,
And without succeeding in the matter for which
I sent it. "For you will go out with joy and be led
forth with peace; the mountains and the hills will
break forth into shouts of joy before you, and all the
trees of the field will clap their hands.
"Instead of the thorn bush the cypress will come up,
And instead of the nettle the myrtle will come up,
And it will be a memorial to the Lord,
For an everlasting sign which will not be cut off."
Isaiah 55:10-13 NASB

Isaiah is revealing the power of God's Word, His instructions, promises, and warnings to produce the transformation needed to walk with God and be empowered through the anointing. God compares His Word as to the rain and snow that falls from heaven and does not return without watering the earth. This rain and snow makes the plants grow and gives seed to the sower.

What makes it rain? First, we will need sunshine. When the sun shines on the water of the earths surface, the heat of the sun turns the water into an invisible gas called vapor. We call this process of changing water into a gas, evaporation. Because the gas is lighter than liquid, the water vapor rises into the sky. Further the gases move up and away from the earths surface, the colder the temperature gets. In the sky the water vapor cools and changes back into tiny water droplets. They call this condensation and is the opposite of evaporation. Clouds are made up of tiny water droplets and so when condensation forms in the sky, clouds form and grow. When water droplets in the cloud bump into each they stick together and grow in size. They continue to grow until they are too heavy and fall as rain. Rain drops even grow as they bump into each other as they journey from the cloud to the earth. Each drop of rain is made up of around one million of the original tiny droplets. We call this the water cycle.

God is giving humanity a natural picture of what it means to walk with God through agreeing with His Word. First of all, God says there must be sunlight that heats the water so that evaporation takes place. I would suggest that we all need the heat of trials to evaporate the things of this world. Peter agrees when he writes in 1 Peter 1:7, the proof of our faith is more precious than gold, though tested by fire, may be found to result in praise and glory and honor at the coming of Jesus.

When we speak of proof, we are talking about evidence that establishes facts. Facts are spoken or written evidence that demand truth through a trial. This proof is the action and process of establishing God's government within the believer. Isaiah is stating a process of changing water into gases. Proverbs 25:4 states that the heat of silver causes the dross to be removed. As we walk in agreement with God's Word, the Holy Spirit removes or evaporates worldly desires and prepares the believer to walk in the anointing.

This evaporation rises above the earth and forms clouds, the vapor then turns back into a million droplets, when the drops reach a certain weight, it rains. This picture is of the believer who undergoes transformation through the renewed mind that walks in agreement with God and then the anointing is poured out. The believer has ventured into a higher atmosphere which transforms vapor into rain. We call this the outpouring of the anointing! Like Psalm 104:30, this believer is the vehicle God uses to renew the face of the earth.

However, not all men can produce. In Jude 1:12, there are men like clouds, visible, but they are without water. Unable to produce seed for the sower and bread for the eater. These waterless believers are swept away by the winds;

here today and gone tomorrow. There is no anointing that waters or renews the face of the earth or mankind, they are swept away like a cloud that produces no rain.

Water is one of the most common symbols for the Holy Spirit and the anointing. Water is indispensable for human life, so there is no lasting life outside of the Holy Spirit. The Apostle John calls this water, living! It is a metaphor for the work of the Holy Spirit in the human heart and out of the belly will come the anointing for works of service or establishing God's Kingdom.

We are talking about walking in agreement with God. Agreement requires faithfulness! This faithfulness produces the cloud or the glory. Nehemiah 9:13-21 tells us of God's faithfulness during the forty years in the wilderness. God gave His Word [law], sent manna from heaven and water from the rock. God led them with the cloud and the pillar. From the glory there will always be fire! Yet Nehemiah says, You gave Your good Spirit to instruct them. Instruction implies agreement and agreement suggests obedience. What is the result? The believer carries the rain that renews, the cloud which is the glory of God, and the fire that makes things pure and true.

Just like rain, snow begins in the clouds! Clouds are tiny water droplets that have evaporated into a gas. Like rain, the heat of the sun evaporates the water, and the gas rises into the sky and then condenses back into water. Remember, tiny water droplets remain in the sky until they are too heavy and then it rains. If the temperatures are warm, it will rain. If the ground temperature is cold enough, the raindrops will freeze but only near the ground, they call this freezing rain. Snow only occurs when the temperatures are freezing all the way from the ground to the clouds.

We see that everything starts from above, so the solution is what comes down, and that is the Word of God. It is God's ways and thoughts through His Word that brings the blessings down. The Word that has gone out of God's mouth is activated by the Holy Spirit and shall accomplish what He desires. Isaiah shows us that God's Word comes in two ways, rain or snow. When it rains, it immediately soaks into the earth, waters it, and makes it fruitful. Snow lies on the hard surface of the earth and does not immediately do anything for it. In fact, the temperature has to change; the sun must shine to melt the snow and make the earth capable of receiving it.

We know that snow melt is more beneficial than ordinary rain. What I am driving at is, God's Word comes to us like rain and we can receive it immediately. God's Word can come into our hearts instantly and produces fruitfulness. But, when God's Word comes as snow, it lies on the hard surface of the earth and does not instantly do anything for it. For snow to be beneficial, the temperature has to change and the sun must shine to melt the snow and make the earth capable of receiving it. The disciples said to Jesus in scripture, this is a hard saying, who can receive it. That is snow! So when God's Word comes as snow, don't reject it, just let it sit on the hard surface of the heart and wait for the Holy Spirit's love and grace to melt it. Only then will our hearts be able to receive it. In fact, the rain and the snow will produce two different products, bread for ourselves and seed for others. Once the Word of God is received into our hearts, we move in faith, and the anointing goes forth.

Psalm 80:18 says, Revive us and we will call on Your name. Once the heart is receivable and responsive to God's Word, the Holy Spirit brings restoration, a conscious towards God, and a Holy Spirit lead life. We are given new strength and energy to service the Lord. Song of Solomon 1:4 says, Draw me away with you and let us run together! To draw is the pull or drag to make it follow behind. It is the Holy Spirit and the anointing that draws us aside for intimacy and fellowship. Sometimes in the believers relationship with the Holy Spirit we don't walk but run, then there are times of walking. The anointing will produce seasons in our life, some are fast seasons and some are slow, but the presence and power of the anointing is there.

AGREEING WITH GOD BRINGS HUNGER

"For you shall go out with joy, And be led out with peace; the mountains and the hills shall break forth into singing before you, And all the trees of the field shall clap their hands. Isaiah 55:12

What is God promising us here? First of all, God is promising joy! As the believer walks with God, abiding in His Word, the anointing will bring the gladness of heart. The believer desires and follows the way of everlasting, grace, peace, mercy and love pour forth from the heart. Before I move on, the anointing can become so overwhelming, that it drives the believer. Secondly, God is promising us peace; peace is the fruit of God's presence and the power of the anointing. One of the name's of Jesus is the Prince of Peace! Third, spontaneous praise will flow from the heart and mouth of the believer as the Word and the Spirit have their way! Isaiah says that the mountains and the hills will start to sing and all the trees of the field will clap their hands. It is the Holy Spirit who produces this amazing life in the believer.

Every believer must have the anointing of the Holy Spirit! The baptism of the Holy Spirit is for us personally, but the anointing is if I may, the baptism on steroids. It is from the anointing that the work of God flows, that is, the acceptable work of God. Look at Isaiah 55:13,

> *Instead of the thorn shall come up the cypress tree, And instead of the brier shall come up the myrtle tree; And it shall be to the LORD for a name, For an everlasting sign that shall not be cut off." Isaiah 55:13*

Isaiah says, the anointing will bring about a change in what it produces. The thorn and the brier bush are barren and unfruitful desert trees, and there is no beneficial use. These types of bushes grow in lands that are not livable. God is telling us that the believer who lives by His Word and develops a relationship with the Holy Spirit will be like the cypress and myrtle tree. The cypress and myrtle are shade trees that begin to transform the nature of the desert. The Holy Spirit will cause the believer to live from His presence and in so doing, the anointing will grow. What I am telling the believer is to live under the active, continuous influence and flow of the anointing.

The Holy Spirit's anointing is not a mystery or something that has been hidden, but was demonstrated by the Trinity. In Acts 10:38, God the Father anointed God the Son with God the Holy Spirit and power. The result of being anointed is power! Habakkuk 3:4 says, His brightness was like the light; He had rays flashing from His hand, And there His power was hidden. What Habakkuk is saying, God's anointing (His power) hides in His presence; so there is power in His presence. Every time God's presence comes, the measure of the presence reveals the measure of the power! The King James Bible uses horns instead of rays, but both mean strength and power of a king. The figurative meaning is granting victory or bestowing prosperity.

This is what Isaiah is saying, our ways and thoughts, our religion and programs produce the thorn and brier bush. But when God's ways and thoughts come, fruitfulness and productivity will be the result. God's Word and the anointing of the Holy Spirit coming into our lives will produce four things, joy, peace, praise, and fruitfulness. Isaiah closes his chapter by stating that the ultimate purpose is for God's glory!

CHANGING OUR THINKING

There is a principle the anointing demands, this is agreeing with God. This is stated very clearly in Amos 3:3,

Can two walk together, unless they are agreed?

We see in the form of a question, agreement is the solution to walking together. We just got done talking about God's thoughts and ways are higher than our thoughts and ways. So absolute surrender to the anointing and the success of the anointing is walking with God. Absolute surrender is the giving up of our life and abandoning the self will. The Church needs to hear the message of an absolute surrender of one's life to God. One of the most helpless feelings in the world is when someone comes to you for help and you cannot help them. In God's Kingdom there is no substitute for the anointing; it is the oil of heaven that fuels the power of God.

Amos is telling us that if we are to walk with God, we must be united and a likeness. Yes, we are to take on the likeness of the Lord Jesus Christ. This is the definition of together! We are to be joined for a common purpose and we are to have common feelings. Yes, God has given us the ability to have feelings, so we too are to have His feelings. Jesus makes this point perfectly, I and the Father are One! God anoints a believer for a purpose, but if we do not harmonize with God in our ways and thoughts, the anointing will lay dormant. Here is the dilemma, our thoughts and ways are not Gods.

Most people settle for the gift! Let us take the gift of leading worship. The worship leader has an amazing voice and when the gift is in use, the presence of God comes, why? Because the gift is from the Father, it is eternal and will always work. Romans 11:29 says,

> *For the gifts and the calling of God are irrevocable [for He does not withdraw what He has given, nor does He change His mind about those to whom He gives His grace or to whom He sends His call].*

God does not withdraw His gift, He created us for these purposes. It was with love He gave the gift, so the believer knows, every time the gift is in operation, it came from the love of the Father. But the anointing is not like the gift! The anointing is for the purposes of God and His work. In Hebrew, the word "anoint" is mashach, which means, "to rub in." The Greek word is chrism and means "to smear." When we receive the anointing, we are "smeared" with His power. The definition hints to an absorbing in of the anointing. We must be surrendered to the call and purposes of God for the anointing to be soaked in. This is where the Christian community gets the phrase "soaking." My point here is if we soak but not transform to what the anointing is driving us too, we will have presence but not power. So someone can use the gift, but to operate in the anointing, one must live a surrendered life.

Since God does not change, the only option left to us is to change our ways and thoughts if we want to harmonize and agree with God. If we understand what the anointing wants, God's purpose, then there comes the acceptance or invitation to walk with God in the anointing. The believer is called to become the anointing! Let me say it this way, the anointing is a power that seeks to drive the one to destiny and purpose. I can't explain the touch or the power of the anointing the day God anointed me. The only explanation I can give is that I was changed into another man.

The anointing went to work on my mind, my interests, my desires were changed and I was driven to serve the Lord. It was a powerful moment. The anointing which is the power of God seeks to work in the believer and upon the believer. Therefore, in the believer for absolute surrender, upon the believer to destroy God's enemies, the kingdom of darkness.

Out of God's grace, He has made provision for us to change. God has given us His Word and the baptism of the Holy Spirit to fulfill that Word. This is an amazing thing God has done for mankind. But God did not stop there, He then released the anointing upon believers, the power of the Holy Spirit who,

> *It shall come to pass in that day that his burden
> will be taken away from your shoulder, and his
> yoke from your neck, and the yoke will be destroyed
> because of the anointing oil. Isaiah 10:27 NKJV*

It is the anointing that will remove the burden from ones shoulders. The Hebrew definition is to remove the weight or load of oppression; what is carried on the shoulders because of forced labor. I can't tell you the thousands of stories when I've seen the anointing set people free and then tell me how their shoulders hurt and how they feel a load has been lifted. The definition for "yoke" is stable gear or device that joins two draft animals at the neck so they can work together as a team; a yoke is an instrument. The anointing will break the oppression; to be forcefully caused to separate into pieces or fragments. When God sets people free from sin, sickness, demons, this oppression is broken into many pieces. The definition points out that oppression is useless because it has been shattered.

Repentance

The Bible has a special word for changing the way we think, it is called repentance. Repentance means literally, to change our mind, that is, to change the way we think. Throughout the New Testament it states this as the primary requirement for reconciliation with God, and the beginning to operate in the anointing. When I come to myself, and understand that I have not been in one mindset with God, I must repent and change my mind. Let me give you an example! I was preaching on the rapture and the second coming of Christ. What I am about to share with you may challenge your belief. I was preaching on pre-tribulation and God clearly spoke to me, "why are you teaching my people wrong." It was the voice, but it was as though I was naked before the Church. That feeling of nakedness happens when one is seeking God but in error. The voice was strong and challenging for repentance. God came to me and literary summoned me to change my mind. I was being tested if you will by God, my leadership for His people needed a new way of thinking. Now the choice was mine! I would like to say that it changed quickly, but that was not the case, it took about a year. Pretribulation is what the Church taught me as a baby Christian, so that is what I believed. But 1 John 2:27 kicked in,

> *But the anointing which you have received from Him abides in you, and you do not need that anyone teach you; but as the same anointing teaches you concerning all things, and is true, and is not a lie, and just as it has taught you, you will abide in Him.*

Remember, we talked about absolute surrender. When the Holy Spirit gave me that feeling of nakedness and that loving voice in that nakedness, it compelled me to change my mind. There is no way for a man in all his ways and thoughts to reconcile with God unless he changes the way he thinks, that is, unless he repents.

> *As it is written in the Prophets: "Behold, I send My messenger before Your face, Who will prepare Your way before You." "The voice of one crying in the wilderness: 'Prepare the way of the LORD ; Make His paths straight.' " John came baptizing in the wilderness and preaching a baptism of repentance for the remission of sins. Mark 1:2-4 NKJV*

Mark is revealing to us, the people of Israel need to change their thoughts and ways if they were going to accept the anointed One, Christ Jesus. John says the way this is to happen is through repentance. Now look at verse 14,15 of Mark 1,

> *Now after John was put in prison, Jesus came to Galilee, preaching the gospel of the king-dom of God, and saying, "The time is ful-filled, and the kingdom of God is at hand. Repent, and believe in the gospel."*

Jesus went into Galilee and proclaimed the good news, the gospel of the Kingdom of God. We must repent and believe the good news, this is to be teachable. The anointing of the Holy Spirit requires a man to be teachable. The very first command Jesus gave in His public ministry is to repent, change the way we think. Only after repentance can a person believe. It is a great error to imagine that we can believe in the true sense of the word believe, until we have repented.

Let me close with this thought, after His resurrection, Jesus told His disciples in Luke 24:47, repentance and for-giveness of sins will be preached in His name to all nations beginning at Jerusalem. Notice the order of the message, repentance first and then the forgiveness of sins. I had to repent for my false belief concerning the tribulation. The Holy Spirit cannot anoint a doctrine of error. Second, the nakedness has to do with sin or error. This happened to Adam and Eve, their error and sin brought nakedness and shame. There was no shame in that encounter I had with the Lord, but exposure. I knew I was in error! The only words that come to mind are what Isaiah said in chapter 6, "Woe is me, for I am undone! Because I am a man of unclean lips, And I dwell in the midst of a people of unclean lips; For my eyes have seen the King, The LORD of hosts."

The nakedness I felt has to do with the definition in Isaiah 6:5, I am undone. The definition is to stop or cease an activity in which one is engaged or be silent, i.e., refrain from making a sound, including speaking or talking. I would like for everyone right now to ask God to send that feeling of nakedness the next time we need to cease activity or stop speaking! In Isaiah 6:7, "Behold, this has touched your lips; Your iniquity is taken away, And your sin purged." This is exactly what the anointing seeks to eliminate, to break the curses of the bloodline known as iniquity and to purge or cleanse the believer's life from sin.

CHAPTER THREE

TAKE HOLD OF GOD'S OBJECTIVES

As we pursue walking with God and the power of the anointing, I have been taking us through some logical steps; some sensible rules if you will that aids and develops the anointing.

But ye shall receive power, after that the
Holy Ghost is come upon you. Acts 1:8

The anointing is God's power and is the manifestation and the result of His presence. As I have said before, there is no substitute for the anointing of God. It is the oil of heaven that empowers the believer to walk with Christ in extreme levels. Yes, we have now graduated to the development stages of the anointing. The anointing has always brought me into new dimensions with the Holy Spirit. So let us look at embracing God's objectives. There are certain area's of our thinking that need to change for the anointing to work effectively. We must consider what is included in that great all-embracing concept of our thoughts. How can we catalog our thoughts that the anointing is activated by? There are thoughts and ways from the Word of God that demands us to learn, so it empowers the anointing.

There are four kinds or ways of thoughts and this is not a complete categorization but a simple base of handling. The four main categories are, first objective, second priority, three attitudes, and four categories. In every one of these areas' we need to learn to think the way God thinks. This is vital for the development of the anointing. If our thoughts were not of importance, God would not have given us His Word to renew our minds.

We must learn to enter into God's objectives. God always has intentions and purposes. There is in most cases a theme if you will as the anointing flows. In healing, there are many healing's that take place, but there will be certain aliments that stick out. Deliverance is the same way, there will be certain evil spirits that God targets and it is designed to show God's people verifiable facts about His Kingdom. These aliments or targeted spirits point out the idea of God's ways and how He thinks. It is the believers responsibility to recognize what God is doing, and to change our way of thinking. The anointing, like I said before, is always teaching, we must see it and transform to it.

From the beginning God has revealed to mankind that His priority has been fellowship. This is clearly demonstrated today in what the Church calls soaking. The anointing is God's power, but the presence is His person. So we must have the presence so that the anointing will work properly. Priority is a fact or condition of being what is regarded and treated as of most importance. Is this how most believers examine the Word of God? We all want to be anointed, but we value our beliefs, thoughts and ways over transforming to God's. We must be able to see God's priorities if we expect the anointing to expand our capacity. Without an increase in the believer's life, that one becomes stagnate and no longer pliable. When this takes place, the believers position in the spirit world diminishes and the anointing seems not to be as effective.

God requires the believer who desires the anointing to walk with Him. This cannot happen unless the believer develops the Godlike attitude. An attitude is a settle way of thinking and feeling about something. For example, we thrive with revelation but we perish without it. The Godlike attitude along with revelation will open to the believer new ways of living, faith, new possibilities and dimensions to the anointing. It was never God's design to live the Christian life without the anointing. I see many believers chasing after the anointing. They are going from one meeting to the next, living life in a big circle, never receiving what they really desire. That believer has not stopped to consider God's objectives and His attitudes.

When we talk about categories, we are speaking about concepts, beliefs, and convictions that form the human mindset. The problem is that most Christians don't tune into God's revelation. It is from the mindset that the anointing flourishes. A mindset is established from desire and correct truth. The Bible gives one of many names to the Holy Spirit as the Spirit of Truth. In John 16:13, "but when He, the Spirit of truth, comes, He will guide you into all the truth." A guide is someone who advises and shows the way. The Bible is intelligible revelations that the Holy Spirit who is the power or anointing is saying and He will operate from that truth. The problem is the believer won't always accept the truth. For example, many say we are not to allow demons to manifest. Yet, that believer does not understand that it is God and God alone that makes the manifestation happen. This is truth! The Bible clearly states that Jesus drove out evil spirits by the finger of God or the Holy Spirit who is the anointing.

The believer who operates in the anointing has learned to perceive the things of God. The one who cannot recognized and grasp the things the anointing is manifesting, he visually sees, but he does not see. He can hear, but he cannot truly hear! The natural man cannot receive the things from the Holy Spirit. I will let the apostle Paul speak to you in this matter,

> *But the natural [unbelieving] man does not accept the things [the teachings and revelations] of the Spirit of God, for they are foolishness [absurd and illogical] to him; and he is incapable*

> *of understanding them, because they are spiritually discerned and appreciated, [and he is unqualified to judge spiritual matters]. 15 But the spiritual man [the spiritually mature Christian] judges all things [questions, examines and applies what the Holy Spirit reveals], yet is himself judged by no one [the unbeliever cannot judge and understand the believer's spiritual nature]. 16 For who has known the mind and purposes of the Lord, so as to instruct Him? But we have the mind of Christ [to be guided by His thoughts and purposes]. 1 Corinthians 2:14-16 Amplified*

The key to be spiritually discerning is to open our spirit man to the truth. This happens when the Holy Spirit is in operation, demonstrating the Word of God. I have spent years of study searching out scriptural truth after the Holy Spirit manifested His power. I spent 10 years investigating the fallen angels after the Holy Spirit brought them down for judgment. The manifestation was for coming revelation. It was also for new levels in the anointing.

> *But as it is written: "Eye has not seen, nor ear heard, nor have entered into the heart of man the things which God has prepared for those who love Him." But God has revealed them to us through His Spirit. For the Spirit searches all things, yes, the deep things of God. 1 Corinthians 2:9-10 NKJV*

The Holy Spirit searches for things that have never been heard by human ears or seen by human eyes. He is the greatest search resource in the entire world. We understand that God's ultimate aim is His own glory and satisfaction. The ultimate purpose of everything in the universe is God's glory and God's satisfaction. This may not sound nice, but a person who does not exist for God's glory and satisfaction does not have the right to exist at all; eternal death supports this conclusion.

God's Objective

I would like to point out some scriptures that clearly reveals God's objective,

> *Oh, the depth of the riches both of the wisdom and knowledge of God! How unsearchable are His judgments and unfathomable His ways! For who has known the mind of the Lord, or who became His counselor? Or who has first given to Him that it might be paid back to him again? For from Him and through Him and to Him are all things. To Him be the glory forever. Amen. Romans 11:33-36 NASB*

Paul says that we can never teach God, in fact it is just the opposite, we need God to teach us. I can never counsel the Lord.

But I do hear Christians say things like "I'm mad at God or why did God let that happen." This kind of thinking shows us that their mind is set on false realities.

CHAPTER THREE

The apostle sings out if you will about the depth and riches of God's wisdom and knowledge that has been given to the Church. Paul quickly states that if one is to come into true revelation, that one is to pursue the mind of God. Since we just read first Corinthians chapter 2, we now know that the Holy Spirit desires for us to have such a deep relationship with God, that for God's glory and His satisfaction, He desires to share His mind with us. The anointing is one powerful way or avenue that God reveals His mind, by His actions.

On February 9 of 1997 a couple of minutes before 2pm, the anointing touched powerfully me. I had been reading a book by Benny Hinn called "The Anointing." How did this take place? First, I exposed myself to the truth. As I continued to read the book, I heard God speaking out of my spirit saying, "you want what he is talking about." As I turned toward the truth, God spoke to me. When I said the prayer at the back of the book, the power of the Holy Spirit fell on me and anointed me. That tangible presence and power stayed with me non-stop for two full years to date. It was God coming to me powerfully and out of that encounter was a mind that desired God and His Word (Truth). That encounter was for His glory and His satisfaction. Since that marvelous day, I have lived to see His glory and to please Him in all I due. This brings satisfaction to the believer, bringing God glory! If the power of God is not flowing, I'm not satisfied, because I feel the Spirit of Truth when He is glorified. It is both an empowering and eternal thing to know that God has been glorified and He is satisfied when we have acted in His behalf.

Paul says, it all comes from God, it all proceeds through God, and it all is consummated in God. This is why Paul states, "For from Him and through Him and to Him are all things. To Him be the glory forever. Amen." Look closely at the ultimate objective, to God be the glory forever! If the reader is now thinking about what I've been writing about, I'm sure you would agree that our minds need to be enlarged so that we can contain deeper realities of the Holy Spirit. One great enemy of happiness, success and fruitfulness is self-centeredness. This is a problem we have by nature, but the presence and power of the Holy Spirit seeks to deliver us. When operating in the anointing, one must be careful not to allow self-centeredness and pride to take root? This will destroy the believer. When man fell from God's grace, man trapped himself in self-esteem.

If we are honest with ourselves, most of us are trapped in self to some degree. Let us look at Psalm 104:30, "May the glory of the Lord endure forever; May the Lord rejoice in His works." Again, what is the aim, God's glory! What will be the outcome, God will rejoice in His work? There is no other higher purpose than to satisfy God. We also see this revelation in Psalm 145:9-11,

The Lord is good to all,
And His tender mercies are over all His works.
All Your works shall praise You, O Lord,
And Your saints shall bless You.
They shall speak of the glory of Your kingdom,
And talk of Your power,

The Church is to speak of the glory of Your Kingdom! How does that happen? As God moves in the power of the Holy Spirit or the anointing. The anointing is releasing God's mercy as He works. Jesus says in John 5:17, "My Father is always at his work to this very day, and I too am working." Jesus the anointed One; Jesus who was anointed without measure. The anointing has a desire to work, and God's people shall bless the Lord as His anointed accomplish the Father's business.

Having predestined us to adoption as sons by Jesus Christ to Himself, according to the good pleasure of His will, to the praise of the glory of His grace, by which He made us accepted in the Beloved. Ephesians 1:5-6 NKJV

Notice God's plan from eternity is called the good pleasure of His will, and it is centered on those who become His children who are accepted through Christ Jesus. If we are accepted in Christ, then we are anointed in Christ. Therefore, Christ the anointed One has anointed all whom God has given Him according to God's pleasure, all to His self-satisfaction and glory. The anointing will always flow from the good pleasure of the Father's will. If there is anything in our life that is not producing glory to God, it is not from His grace.

So that we who were the first to hope in Christ [who first put our confidence in Him as our Lord and Savior] would exist to the praise of His glory. Ephesians 1:12 AMP

Everything that results out of our trusting in Christ for salvation, operating in the anointing, and all other gifts is intended to be for the praise of God's glory. We know that obedience to God is for our good, but it is for the praise of His glory. It is the anointing that brings about God's good, but all the works done under the anointing is God's glory. There is a powerful scripture that brings this point out so clearly.

> *"Worthy are You, our Lord and God, to receive the glory and the honor and the power; for You created all things, and because of Your will they exist, and were created and brought into being." Revelation 4:11*

The Apostle John gives us a list in which we see that God's first objective is His glory, then His honor, and His power. We see that God's glory and honor must come before His power. Those who seek to operate in the anointing must understand this principle. I learned this year's ago when driving home from a meeting. God said, "are you going to thank Me for what I did tonight?" I instantly praised Him for what He did and thanked Him for His righteousness.

How is God's glory, honor, and power brought about? The second part of the verse explains, the ultimate purpose of creation is for God's pleasure. When the Church is taking part in God's plan it pleases Him. It is the will of God that all mankind be saved. So when we operate in the anointing, salvation must be on the top of the list. Therefore, I enjoy power evangelism so much; I can operate in the anointing to bring about salvation. Let us not forget that God create us for His glory, purpose, and His pleasure.

If there is a lack of the anointing in your life, it should concern you. Remember, the presence is not the anointing. The anointing is the power of God to bring Him glory and honor. The question should now be, how are you going to respond for the lack of supernatural power in your life? If you are experiencing a shortage in the anointing, it is a warning you should examine your life. The believer in Christ Jesus should never be on the verge of having their lamp go out! Let the Church get back to God's presence and let the anointing of the Holy Spirit be the focus of the Church along with God's Word. The Church must embrace certain values that bring about the anointing. The culture of the Church has missed the three main goals of creation, God's glory, His honor, and His power; this brings God pleasure. There is no higher objective in living than giving God pleasure; that God may find satisfaction in our lives, that is the highest aim we could ever entertain.

I have heard it said, faith does not come from doing all one can but faith comes from surrender. I am not sure that is totally true. I cannot have faith if I cannot understand or if I don't know something exists, but I can live a surrendered life. God is looking for those who have a yielded heart for sure, for it is with the heart one believes. But before my heart can believe, God must introduce me to eternal realities outside my experiences. This is the design of the anointing. Let me give you an example. The Holy

Spirit introduced me to demonic deliverance back in 1998. I joined a ministry team outside the organized Church because most churches will not embrace all forms of deliverance. They are okay with things like sozo, but directly confronting the demonic or to break generational curses back to Adam, most reject it. It was my willingness to take hold of direct confrontation that brought me 5 years later into an encounter with a fallen angel. When you are anointed for a function, it is God's good pleasure to raise you up to the realms of Christ Jesus. Not that we will ever attain, but Paul ascended to the heights he could list the levels of the second heaven. The anointing depends on a persons humility and their willingness to be trained.

The Objective of the Anointing

The faith of a believer has its origin in the nature, presence, and promises of God. It is the anointing that will bring deeper revelation of God's promises and His nature. God's presence is the fuel for the anointing, but as 1 John 2:27 says, it is the anointing that will teach. So faith results from having the anointing make an impact on the heart. The fruit of a believer's life is to learn how to abide in the anointing. The believer is to grow in the knowledge of God through His Word, His presence, and the anointing will remain active. When I can agree with God, heaven then comes to earth through the anointing. Walking with God is what Adam did in the garden before the fall. When it was time to name the animals, God said rightfully so! The anointing is empowered through agreeing with God; this is walking with God.

CHAPTER THREE

I have also heard it said, the presence of the Lord positions us for miracles, this to is an incomplete revelation. I have seen the presence of God heal and deliver, but I have found that it is the anointing operating through spiritual wisdom and knowledge that brings a greater impact. I have experienced tremendous Holy Spirit presence, but did not see the power. I also have been wrecked by the presence, but the power did not come out of me. Walking with God through agreement is the key to the power. In His presence I experience realms of love, but when the anointing comes, the realms of power open up. To operate in those realms effectively, I must know how the Kingdom of God functions. For example, a lady came to the ministry in dire need of a miracle. Her blood was thickening and the doctors could not help her. The Holy Spirit spoke and said, it is the second heaven that holds her healing. I asked the Lord to send down the fallen angel that has the legal right to her healing. Once the ministry session was over, she was instantly healed. Understanding and walking with God will change your life and ministry forever!

If we are to lead people into the promises of God, it will be through spiritual wisdom and knowledge empowered by the anointing. God's presence will require something from us, but the anointing will drive us to that assignment. Once the anointing came on Jesus at His baptism, He was driven to the wilderness to defeat the kingdom of darkness.

If God is with us, who can be against us? This verse is deeper than it appears. When God is with us, we are expected and enabled to overcome the kingdom of darkness.

That tells me, I must have the presence, God with me, and I must have the anointing, God's power upon me.

What is the objective of the anointing? I will let Acts 10:38 explain it to you.

how God anointed Jesus of Nazareth with the Holy Spirit and with great power; and He went around doing good and healing all who were oppressed by the devil, because God was with Him.

CHAPTER FOUR

EMBRACING GOD'S OBJECTIVE

In our discussion thus far, we have discovered that God invites us to walk with Him and that is the fellowship that God desires to have with man. This means we will have to agree with God. Remember, in Amos 3:3, "Can two walk together, unless they agree?" I have also stressed how we walk with God is key to operating in the anointing. To agree means to harmonize by bringing our ways and thoughts into alignment with God's. We also have discovered that repentance will be a lifestyle. I am repenting when my ways and thoughts don't line up with God's. This is the first step, to reconcile my ways and thoughts so that the anointing may flow unimpeded. As long as our ways and thoughts are not in harmony with God, we are not fully reconciled to God. Therefore, we must live in repentance, that sanctification process bringing us into aliment with God.

When we repent and desire to change our way of thinking, the Bible has a word for this, it is called meditation. The only way to change our minds is to reflect, concentrate, study and pray concerning the scriptures. The Bible reveals God's law, God's Word and God's thoughts. Why is mediating on God's Word so important? Because it brings God's favor and blessing. This is an essential key in operating in the anointing. We have learned that there are four main headings in which we are required to change our thinking so that the anointing may move powerfully. They are, objective, priority, attitude and category.

We discovered in chapter 3 that God's ultimate objective is His satisfaction and glory. We reflected on this by looking at Revelation 4:11, "You are worthy, O Lord, to receive glory and honor and power; for You created all things, and by Your will they exist and were created."

Now we are moving to what I believe is next in line to bring about the power of the anointing, it is excellence! The definition of the Greek noun says, "the excellence of a person or thing that enables it to achieve its end or purpose; especially of moral excellence. When excellence is spoken of as a quality, it means the quality of excelling; possessing good qualities in a high degree. The Bible references excellence as morality, holiness, faithfulness and impressiveness. From an example of this, let us turn back to the Genesis account of creation. Let me point out to you that divine inspection followed every major stage of creation. God inspected His own work, and only when He was satisfied with His work did He move on to His next project.

In the perfection of creation the Holy Spirit was already moving, He was moving before God said. This is of vital importance! Today we know this movement as God's presence. The Spirit of God making Himself known to His people through His presence or we could say, His attendance.

> *Then God said, "Let there be light"; and there was light. And God saw the light, that it was good; and God divided the light from the darkness. God called the light Day, and the darkness He called Night. So the evening and the morning were the first day. Genesis 1:3,4 NKJV*

I think it best before looking at our scripture we define the Hebrew word "move." It means to hover, but the primitive root; to brood; by implication, to be relaxed: — flutter, move, shake. I have seen these manifestations as the presence of God fills the Church. The Holy Spirit is always moving. It was the Holy Spirit that raised Jesus from the dead, and I would suggest that He would like to raise places in us from the dead. My point here is that God starts somewhere and will end somewhere. This is good news for the believer whom the anointing has fallen upon.

In our scripture, notice God examined the light after He had created it. He said it was good! He said it has desirable or positive qualities; especially those suitable for a thing specified. The light according to the "Lemmas" is pleasant, desirable, in order, kind and morally good. This is what the Holy Spirit created from, He was moving, but creation came from good qualities. This too is the product of the anointing.

In Genesis 1:10, "God called the dry land earth, and the gathering of the waters He called seas; and God saw that this was good (pleasing, useful) and He affirmed and sustained it." It satisfied God, the land and the seas. He saw that they were good. Good in the Hebrew means, be in a state of having proper characteristics or performing an expected function. This is the product of the anointing, having genuine and essential qualities that produce God expected functions. The anointing of God is expressed or released from us in all life and ministry that is truly pleasing to Him. Every time we minister in His name, declaring His truth, serving with His heart and demonstrating His power, there is an anointing that goes forth from us. We can see as we trace through the creation account, the anointing or the power of God was creating, examining, and pronouncing that all was good. This is what the anointing does!

Messiah in Old Testament times is a person set apart for a divinely appointed office, such as a king or a priest, was anointed with oil in a sacred rite. The word Messiah is a transliteration of the Hebrew word "anointed" and was translated into Greek as Christos (also meaning "anointed"). In time the term came to refer specifically to the expected king who would deliver God's people, judge the wicked, and usher in God's kingdom. From the creation to the final day of this evil age, Jesus the anointed One has been anointing generations to bring about God's glory and His satisfaction.

> *For we are His workmanship [His own master work, a work of art], created in Christ Jesus [reborn from above—spiritually transformed, renewed, ready to be used] for good works, which God prepared [for us] beforehand [taking paths which He set], so that we would walk in them [living the good life which He prearranged and made ready for us]. Ephesians 2:10 AMP*

As we walk with God, He brings us into a state of having proper characteristics and performing expected functions through the power of the anointing. As God created the heavens and the earth and He saw that it was good, He has created us and anointed us for good works. We are what He has made, a new creation in Christ (Anointed One) Jesus. This new creation is spiritually transformed and going through transformation, that is, taking paths which lead us into our created purpose and destiny through the works of the anointing. If we are to walk in the paths God created for us to walk in, first, we must learn to walk with God. Second, it will be the anointing that reveals these paths or purposes to us.

The anointing is for a work, a spiritual task that God has called us too in Christ or in the Anointed One. These tasks birthed in the new creation are designed to be normal job assignments. This is what the word definition means, normal works of business. If we don't endeavor in these works through the anointing, we are not doing business for the Kingdom of God. The question then is, how do we find these assignments?

For all who are allowing themselves to be led by the
Spirit of God are sons of God. Romans 8:14 AMP

Sometimes the amplified can be so illuminating. I like this translation because it describes those who are allowing the Holy Spirit to lead them into the power of the new creation and the works of the anointing. To allow means giving someone permission to do something. This is how we find the callings and purposes of the anointing. I must allow the Holy Spirit to lead me! To be led is a willful undergoing of an action or course of action because of a moral and spiritual influence. We must notice the word moral here. It is an influence when the believer is seeking the anointing and also a power when the anointing comes upon him. The influence of the Holy Spirit is directly tied to morality. Willful sin is an enemy to one's anointing, just look at Samson's life.

There is a willful undergoing of action. I must be intentional and strong-willed in pursuing the anointing. The touch or the supernatural empowerment is only a beginning; it is the starting point. I must be deliberate in my pursuit! The second part to the definition is an important point that most miss. The course of action determines the depth of the anointing. I can pursue the training, but who

I am trained by is everything! We must be lead to our minister. There will be key foundations that must be learned. More than likely, you will do the things your teacher does, but from your anointing. The student must also understand the course of action will take them beyond their teacher.

We must allow the training and the working out of that training have its way in us. Therefore, we must become the anointing. It must be a driving force within us. I love the fire of God, His healing power and the casting out of evil spirits. This is my anointing. I love it and desire to see more of it. As God did with the creation in Genesis 1, the creation had to pass God's inspection, His standard of excellence. It is that way with the anointing. Until we have reached a standard of knowledge and excellence in the anointing, God will not promote us in the anointing. People want to move on before they fully develop their anointing. This too is an enemy of the anointing. It is God who anoints, and it is He who promotes.

At the end of Genesis 1, God saw everything He had made, and behold, it was superb and He validated it completely. This is the course of action God desires us to go through. This reveals an important principle for us, each step will be good, but as the whole, it will be fantastic. Every step of the anointing must come to its fullest and over time, we will look at each step as vital to the person who moves in the anointing. Therefore, the principle is that the whole is more than the sum of the parts. Every step along the way was good, but when every learning experience is brought together, in harmony with God's design and His purpose, the completed whole far exceeded the individual steps. Each step, phase and experience was good, but the completion of the anointing brings God glory and satisfaction.

We must understand the goal of the anointing; to bring God glory and show His excellence. This is how the anointing comes to its highest potential. When I am in a deliverance room, after 22 years of training and encounters, I can get done more and in less time than one who has been casting out demons for only 5 years. I see more people healed because I tell them what I know, that we must meet spiritual conditions before healing will flow. To remain anointed, one must speak in love, but also in truth. Most believers don't want to hear the hard things, but it is the telling of the hard things that will bring them breakthrough.

Let me just comment on the true nature of sin. Sin in its essence is failure to achieve the objective of creation, God's glory and His excellence as in Genesis. I would now submit, the true carnal nature of man will cause the anointing not to reach its objective that brings God glory and reveals His excellence. If we don't see this principle in its context, we will always have an incomplete and superficial concept of what the anointing really is. Therefore, sin is failing to achieve the two primary objectives of the Creator, first His own glory and second, His excellence. This principle must be applied to the anointing.

This is so simply stated in Romans 3:23, "since all have sinned and continually fall short of the glory of God." As I mentioned before, sin and the carnal nature is the enemy of the anointing. The nature of sin falls short of God's glory and will work against the anointing. I have used the words "work against." It is the anointing that does the work, but it is the sin nature in humanity that will want not to yield. That sin nature will work and cause us to not meet God's standard of excellence He has called us too; God's work through the anointing in us. So, sin in its essence is leading a life that robs God of His glory and fails to achieve His standard of excellence.

Now let us look at Abraham as our pattern of true believers in Romans 4:20-22,

> *But he did not doubt or waver in unbelief concerning the promise of God, but he grew strong and empowered by faith, giving glory to God, being fully convinced that God had the power to do what He had promised. Therefore his faith was credited to him as righteousness (right standing with God).*

It is not perfection that God is looking for, that we have in Christ Jesus. What God is looking for in the believer is for us to bring God glory. Abraham gave glory to God by fulfilling the purpose of the Creator. How did he do it? By his faith! He could not do it by morality and righteousness, because we have all sinned. But out of Abraham's sin, he turned to God in faith and believing God could do what He promised; he gave glory to God. We too like Abraham must fulfill our purpose. To go through the Christian life and not move in the anointing's power is not impacting earth and bringing God glory. Notice in the scripture, faith gives back to God the glory which sin has robbed Him. Likewise, unbelief or not answering the call and receiving the anointing will continue to rob God of His glory.

Paul says, through faith it enables us to achieve excellence. I like that word "enables." Mounces' Complete Dictionary defines the anointing as, "usually refers to pouring or smearing sacred oil on a person in a ceremony of dedication, possibly symbolizing divine empowering to accomplish the task or office." The anointing empowered by faith enables us to achieve God's desires for our life.

In 2 Peter 1:5 we read, "For this very reason, make every effort to add to your faith goodness; and to goodness, knowledge." The word goodness translated there, basically throughout the Greek language up to that time, is normally translated excellence. Some translations say moral excellence, but it is not complete in meaning. Yes, we need moral excellence to operate in the anointing, but it also requires faith through works and assignments. God wants excellence in every area, that was His standard at the creation and that is also what Paul and Peter are driving at. The wonderful truth about faith in God is that it actives the anointing and it brings about power to do what God has promised. Then out of that faith and the operation of the anointing we add excellence. So faith and the anointing achieves the two purposes which sin failed to achieve, God's glory and it enables us to achieve God's standard of excellence.

Embracing God's Priorities

Let me highlight what we have been discussing in this book! For the power of the anointing to be effective, we must learn to walk with God. To walk with God means we must agree with God. To agree with God, we must bring our ways and thoughts into aliment with God. The way we can do this is by receiving God's Word into our hearts and minds. God's Word brings His ways and thoughts down from heaven into the earth. The key response of the believer is to undergo a change of thinking through a lifestyle of repentance. There are four main areas in which we must change our thinking, first objectives, second priorities, third attitudes and fourth categories. We have just discussed God's objectives, so let us move on to God's priorities.

Now we understand the anointing moves in authority and power when God is glorified, and when He is satisfied. This brings out excellence through the anointing. What is God's priorities? This is of tremendous importance if we desire to grow in the anointing. If our priorities are not in-line with God, we cannot agree with Him and the anointing is less effective. Let me suggest that God's first priority has its center in His Kingdom. What I mean is God desires to bring His Kingdom into being on earth. Many Christians are desiring to go to heaven and that is important. But while we are here on earth, we should live to see God's Kingdom here on earth. This happens as believers seek to bring God's presence and power into the earth. God works through the anointing!

The Bible teaches that God wants heaven and earth to be one, and this will happen as God closes out this evil age. Believers are to transform their thinking, give up this earthly life, and agree with God; walking with Him through the power of the anointing establishing God's kingdom on earth. Let us look at Matthew 6:9-10 NKJV,

In this manner, therefore, pray: Our Father in heaven, Hallowed be Your name. Your kingdom come. Your will be done on earth as it is in heaven.

Jesus told His disciples how to pray and set a pattern for prayer. Jesus tells us many things to pray for in scripture, but we are talking about God's first priority. This model has a few priorities listed. Jesus says we must establish a relationship in prayer with the Father. We clearly see this in, our Father in heaven. Notice He is also talking about corporate prayer by using the word "our." When Jesus moves to "hallowed be Your name," this involves identifying with God's objective of His own glory. Then we are to go on, "Your kingdom come." In praying this we are identifying ourself with God's priority in the affairs of earth. Jesus closes the pattern of prayer by revealing where the action is here on earth.

We are living today for an exodus from the earth, but through the anointing bringing the tangible reality of heaven to earth. This happens when God's will is brought about on earth as it is in heaven. Can you believe that God's will can be done in your life? What if every Christian lived for His will in their life? I would suggest that we would see a different world. As I said before, the anointing drives me to preach the gospel, bring healing to the sick, and to deliver the oppressed by expelling demons out of all people. People give glory to God when I yield to the anointing and watch the excellence of God, bringing Him satisfaction.

Jesus returns to this priority later on in Matthew 6:33 NKJV,

> *But seek first the kingdom of God and His right-eousness, and all these things shall be added to you.*

It is God's presence that transforms our hearts. We come to know His ways as we spend time in His presence. God will only reveal His ways to those who know Him. Once we see His way, then it is our responsibility to understand His thoughts. The thoughts of God come in a couple of ways. First that still soft voice like someone is speaking to you from behind. The second way is the constant thought or picture that won't go away. Third is the unction or what my wife has labelled as the knower, you know that you know. Then there is the power of God. Fourth is when the power of God is manifesting, God is speaking to all who are watching.

Jesus says we are to seek the Kingdom of God, again this is the first priority. Seeking is a search for or to try to get or reach something one desires. This is where the anointing is so powerful. When we operate in the anointing prioritizing the search and desire of the manifested presence and power of God, His Kingdom comes and His will is done.

At times we can put our personal ambitions and eagerness before the Kingdom or we can put them before the timing of God. This too will cause the anointing to not operate at a high level. Jesus says, the priority for all believers is to put the coming of God's Kingdom first. This is what the children of God must embrace! I see a lot of believers performing or playing Church. They function out of their gift and not out of the anointing. If the believer's life exhibits no power, there is no anointing, just a gift. Most of the Church put their own personal needs and plans ahead of the Kingdom. These believers desiring to be used by God rarely are and are okay with just desire.

Let us move on to what I believe is the second major priority of God, the eternal before the temporal. God has always put the priority of the eternal before the temporal. We can see now what God designed the anointing to do a little better by stating that He requires the eternal be put before the temporal. We always must absorb in mind that which God places as ultimate importance. God will not sacrifice one moment of eternity for time or age. We see this in the temptation of Jesus. The Bible clearly teaches that the value of the smallest part of eternity cannot compare with all of time rolled up together. I'm sure you are thinking about Paul's writings to the Corinthian Church,

For our light affliction, which is but for a mo-

> *ment, is working for us a far more exceeding*
> *and eternal weight of glory, while we do not look*
> *at the things which are seen, but at the things*
> *which are not seen. For the things which are seen*
> *are temporary, but the things which are not seen*
> *are eternal. 2 Corinthians 4:17-18 NKJV*

Paul is telling the Corinthian Church that there are two kinds of things that enter the human life, the temporary and the eternal. The believer who operates in the anointing has the mindset of overcoming the temporal with the eternal.

Paul knew that the hardships he went through were microscopic and wouldn't last long compared to how long he would enjoy eternity—the immeasurably great glory that will last forever. What really matters—what is eternal and permanent—cannot be seen, touched, or measured. But this scripture is deeper than most understand it to be. The Kingdom of God has come, the eternal has invaded the temporal. Even if our bodies experience trials and tribulations in the temporal, our minds and spirit can encounter the eternal. We are called to exercise the eternal over the temporal through the gifts of the Holy Spirit and the powerful presence of the anointing.

The scripture states God is working in us His eternal purposes in this temporal world. This only happens according to Paul as long as we look at the eternal and not the temporal. I have also found if a believer could see themselves healed or delivered, the power of the anointing would set them free. There is a reality here that we can't miss, it is, where we focus our attention makes all the difference in how God can deal with us.

And we know that all things work together for good to those who love God, to those who are the called according to His purpose. Romans 8:28 NKJV

Paul says, in all that God does in our lives it will work for the good. We have been talking about the power of the anointing and walking with God. This is the necessary requirement for all things to work together for the good. We must walk with God in agreement, it is His will here that will be done. Notice it is God who is orchestrating the believer's life as that one follows the callings and purposes of God. God is always working for the good, this is where the anointing manifests. God anointed Jesus, and He went about doing good. So God's primary aim is releasing His goodness and establishing His standard of excellence in this temporal age.

In our growth and our walking with God, experiencing the power of the anointing, we must focus on what God is doing now in our lives. We will not move on to the next phrase or season in our life until God has established excellence in the season we are in. This is a reality that very few believers pay attention too. The believer wants more from God, yet they do not establish God's excellence in themselves for the season they are in. So, if you are a servant of God, understand this, there will be no new season until God is satisfied by creating His excellence in our life. This is what Paul is alluding too, an eternal excellence that far out weights the things of the temporal. Yes, God wants the eternal to manifest over the temporal. This excellence and moral goodness stands the test of eternity; something that will not fade or wither; something that will pass through the fire and have an eternal weight in eternity.

We now realize that whatever happens in time is of secondary importance in shaping our eternal character; for what we are in our character is eternal.

CHAPTER FIVE

FOCUSING ON GOD'S PRIORITIES

I would like to open this chapter with a quick review on how the power of the anointing works. The anointing is not the baptism of the Holy Spirit, but a ceremonial setting apart to God for a special task. It is an empowerment that opens up the spirit realm. The anointing instantly activates gifts, callings and teaches us. If we have the anointing, it drives us to study the Bible and our gifts. This anointing begins when we understand that through the gospel it invites us to walk with God. We found out that to do this we will have to agree with God. If we have the same opinion with God, then we are in harmony with God. To be in harmony with God, we must become a friend of God. This requires a total different way of thinking. Finally, in the last chapter I listed four main areas that must be addressed for a change of ways and thoughts.

In the last chapter we covered God's objectives and His two primary dealings with the universe; His own glory and satisfaction and secondly excellence. The anointing of the Holy Spirit will seek to give God glory and satisfaction through His excellence. Like the creation, God saw it was very good or excellent, that is what the anointing desires to do. To take the believer through an orderly process to achieve God's ultimate goal.

In this chapter I would like to begin with the second category, God's priorities. Unless our priorities are inline with God's, the anointing will not be effective and we cannot walk with God. We see in Psalm 103:7 that God made known His ways to Moses, but Israel chose only to know God's acts. Moses found the secret to operating in the anointing, to know God and understand what God desired of him. God will only reveal His ways and thoughts to those who walked in agreement with Him. When we know God ways and thoughts, it focus us on His priorities in the earth. We will not live for our priorities, but His. There is a powerful transformation waiting for the believer who choses to put God's priorities first. Do you know what God's primary concerns are?

When we look at God's first priority, He centers it on His Kingdom. What I am saying is, in all of God's dealings with the world and humanity, His main priority is to bring His kingdom into being on earth as it is in heaven. If the churches main priority was to bring God's Kingdom to earth, God's person, His presence and His glory would be more clear in the earth. The one who teaches the believer that through the anointing we must release God's presence and power, he has God's priorities in mind. It is the anointing that transforms the nature of man and causes that believer to release that nature. We could say, the anointing upon the believer changes the character within that believer. The anointing works delicately or secretly in our hearts until it is the time for activation. When we activate the anointing, it seeks to destroy darkness, bring a breakthrough to the oppressed and becomes aggressive toward sickness and disease.

Let us look at 1 Samuel 10 for some helpful truths about the anointing. In verse one, Samuel took the flask of oil and poured it on Saul's head, kissed him, and said, "Has the Lord not anointed you as ruler over His inheritance (Israel)? The very first thing we learn about the anointing is the person who is doing the anointing ceremony must be anointed. Kings were set apart through the ritual of anointing; a prophet who acted in God's power and authority performed the ceremony. According to Isaiah 61:1, the anointing was to authorize and set apart, a person for a particular work or service. The Old Testament reveals that the anointed person belonged to God in a special sense. The phrases, "the Lord's anointed," "God's anointed," "My anointed," "Your anointed," or "His anointed" are used.

The next powerful truth about the anointing is that sacred oil is used and poured over the person's head. This is a symbol for the Holy Spirit coming upon someone. I remember that day, the supernatural heat that came down my head and over my body. Instantly, I was activated for service, empowered by God's Spirit and given a gift. Immediately came the voice of God saying, "you must respect your enemy and you must be fully trained." With King Saul, he was given authority over God's people. When the believer receives the anointing, it gives them authority over for a particular task. But authority over does not mean that believer knows how to rule. This is where training comes into play. When we know how God operates and how the kingdom of darkness works, the power of the anointing flows. When the anointing came upon my wife, intercession immediately came out of her. The Spirit of the Lord came upon her and uncontrollable travail came forth. Today, she at times can control travail and then there are other times when travail is uncontrollable. It is presumptive or the absence of spiritual knowledge that one would think they could control the Holy Spirit who is praying. I laugh at the one who thinks they have everything under control by quoting the scripture, the spirits of prophets are subject to prophets, 1 Corinthians 14:32. Yes, it works in the prophetic realm, but with intercession, God reserves the right. Anyone who thinks differently needs to hang around a different level of intercession.

Just a few verses down, we see Samuel prophesy that the Spirit of the LORD would come powerfully upon Saul, and he would prophesy with the prophets. Samuel tells Saul that he would be changed into a different person. There are times the anointing will make us very bold. It seems to influence the character of the individual and even that one's behavior. Smith Wigglesworth for example would physically kick and hit, but the power to heal would flow. Anyone who seeks to become one with the anointing will experience character and behavior encounters with the Holy Spirit at times. The operation of the gift of faith often is the source of this encounter.

I remember going to Colombia South America with a minister who back then held an event called the "Transformation Summit." Because of beliefs and certain training techniques, the power of the Holy Spirit would be restrained. The same is true with a ministry out of Pennsylvania who goes into Brazil. We must understand that the Holy Spirit cannot be controlled, but we also must not allow fleshly impulses that cause crazy behavior. Why did people accept Smith Wigglesworth punching people in the stomach and so forth, because God healed. If God was not in it, God would not of healed. Do not be religious here, I've done unusual stuff that has moved God and also things that have been void of power. I will state it again as I did a few pages ago, "we could say, the anointing upon the believer changes the character within that believer." So God's priorities are bringing heaven to earth and God always values the eternal over the temporal.

Partaking of God's Attitudes

We have talked in the last part of chapter four about how God works with eternity in view. I would like to mention Romans 5:2-5 before we move on to partaking of God's attitudes.

Through Him we also have access by faith into this [remarkable state of] grace in which we [firmly and safely and securely] stand. Let us rejoice in our hope and the confident assurance of [experiencing and enjoying] the glory of [our great] God [the manifestation of His excellence and power]. And not only this, but [with joy] let us exult in our sufferings and rejoice in our hardships, knowing that hardship (distress, pressure, trouble) produces patient endurance; and endurance, proven character (spiritual maturity); and proven character, hope and confident assurance [of eternal salvation]. Such hope [in God's promises] never disappoints us, because God's love has been abundantly poured out within our hearts through the Holy Spirit who was given to us.

The writer of the Bible who is the Holy Spirit continually has different authors talk to us about gaining knowledge and understanding. Through these revelations we would understand what really matters. For example, we should have the ability to differentiate between right and wrong, good and evil, eternal and temporal, and we should have discernment to decide what is morally excellence and holy. Paul spells out to the Philippians these very things, so that they could choose those things that are more valuable. What is of eternal value that brings godly moral character and holiness? Is it not the Holy Spirit and the work of His anointing. So God is working for our eternal state in view. When He is dealing with us, God works all things for our eternal good to make us the best kind of person in character throughout eternity.

With that said, I would now like to talk about God's attitudes. This has been one of the toughest subjects for me. When things are not going as I planned, I then get to look at myself and evaluate whether I have God's attitude or my own. God's attitude about this temporal world that is passing away is vital for the transformation of our thoughts and ways. It is essential in the anointing's development. So let us talk about infinite attention to detail. Very few Christians ever consider or I could say ignore this attitude of God. God has the same attitude if something is big or if it small. Your anointing is of the same value because it comes from the Holy Spirit. Tell yourself right now, my calling, purpose and anointing is of eternal value. This eternal attitude is so clearly seen in Luke 16:10, God attention is on the small and the large.

He who is faithful in a very little thing is also faithful in much; and he who is dishonest in a very little thing is also dishonest in much.

I would like to ask you, are you faithful in the very little? If you are, then God sees that you will be faithful and responsible with much. My point here is, everything God has established, from the stars in the sky to the grains of sand on the beach, each exhibits the same principle, the wisdom of God. It is not what we consider little or great, no matter what the size, everything comes from the wisdom and understanding of God. This is the power of the anointing. From the smallest of healings or deliverances, to the raising of the dead or dealing with Satan himself in deliverance, in all things it displays God's glory and wisdom.

Therefore, God does not have the attitude if it is big then it is of importance. God does not decrease His care if something is smaller. There was a minister who came to my Church and said something that made no sense. He said, I will send people your way that has an "A" class anointing. He had overlooked the Luke 16:10 passage where Jesus explains all things to him are of vital importance. Did that minister even contact me, NO! If there is no eternal focus, then empty promises are made.

Today I pastor a church of about fifty people, but I am also the author of "Exploring Secrets of the Heavenly Realms" series. The most advanced book on spiritual warfare and territorial spirits. I can say, as of May 2019, there is not a book series in print that is as advanced as this on that subject. My comment here is, who can know or understand God's wisdom and power. With the information given in Exploring Secrets of the Heavenly Realms, the Church is spiritually ready for the end time harvest and the sanctification of the saints.

I do understand there is another way of looking at Luke 16:10 in regards to worldly wealth. How people handle their worldly wealth shows their trustworthiness. If a person can be trusted with a little bit, if he or she maintains integrity even in small matters, then that person has proven trustworthiness for large matters. The reverse is also true—the one who would willingly steal a dollar may also be willing to steal thousands. Trustworthiness goes to a person's very core.

But the subject is God's attitude! Both examples equally apply, yet one focus' on us, the other on God. Can you trust God now to go to great lengths to bring about your vision and desires? The secret to moving in a higher level of the anointing is to be faithful with the anointing we have today. Oh, the glory and presence of God!

It is not the size of our ministry or the power of God in our ministry that will have an eternal weight or how we will live in eternity, but how faithful we serve and the character we display. The minute we look at something from the lens of the temporal, we have not seen the wisdom and glory of God in that matter. When God anoints, He will always check on us through the little things. Mostly, these checks come through trials! The trial comes to examine our heart. This is where we turn to God's presence and power. This is where the believer will say, "I will trust You Oh Lord, for You have my eternal state in mind."

Therefore, God examines the littlest of things in our lives, and one tool God uses is the anointing. The Luke 16:10 principle is, if we are not faithful in the little things, we cannot be trusted with that which is great. Again, we are not talking about the size of ministry or the power in which we operate, but the eternal secrets of heaven that effect the whole creation. Therefore, I established "Kingdom Mysteries Publishing," publishing those things that are eternal and of heavenly value.

One thing I've found with the person who operates from the gift and not the anointing, they promote themselves. They can climb the ladder of success, but they can never achieve God's promotion. Just because we have big ministries or we have hit some financial breakthrough, does not mean God's blessing is on it. People will follow a good speaker, but unless the power of God is moving consistently, the gift is in operation and not the anointing.

"For the kingdom of heaven is like a man traveling to a far country, who called his own servants and delivered his goods to them. And to one he gave five talents, to another two, and to another one, to each according to his own ability; and immediately he went on a journey. Then he who had received the five talents went and traded with them, and made another five talents. And likewise he who had received two gained two more also. But he who had received one went and dug in the ground, and hid his lord's money. After a long time the lord of those servants came and settled accounts with them.

"So he who had received five talents came and brought five other talents, saying, 'Lord, you delivered to me five talents; look, I have gained five more talents besides them.' His lord said to him, 'Well done, good and faithful servant; you were faithful over a few things, I will make you ruler over many things. Enter into the joy of your lord.' He also who had received two talents came and said, 'Lord, you delivered to me two talents; look, I have gained two more talents besides them.' His lord said to him, 'Well done, good and faithful servant; you have been faithful over a few things, I will make you ruler over many things. Enter into the joy of your lord.'

"Then he who had received the one talent came and said, 'Lord, I knew you to be a hard man, reaping where you have not sown, and gathering where you have not scattered seed. And I was afraid, and went and hid your talent in the ground. Look, there you have what is yours.'

"But his lord answered and said to him, 'You wicked and lazy servant, you knew that I reap where I have not sown, and gather where I have not scattered seed. So you ought to have deposited my money with the bankers, and at my coming I would have received back my own with interest. So take the talent from him, and give it to him who has ten talents.

'For to everyone who has, more will be given, and he will have abundance; but from him who does not have, even what he has will be taken away. And cast the unprofitable servant into the outer darkness. There will be weeping and gnashing of teeth.'

MATTHEW 25:14-30 NKJV

The first thing I want to point out is that God will settle accounts, each of us according to our ability. The word ability means the quality of being able to perform; especially a quality that permits or facilitates achievement or accomplishment. Therefore, God has given each of us the ability to perform a particular activity or to undergo some experience or trial. Notice the order, faithful in the few before being put in charge of many. This is the power of the anointing! God authorize's talent and anoints the believer with power and strength to achieve, but it is up to us to act upon for success.

God attaches tremendous importance to being faithful, we see this with the wicked servant. The servant with the one talent had not been faithful in the little, he considered his talent unimportant. This principle is a Kingdom rule, faithfulness to the anointing and the call of God is of great value. A talent is a Greek monetary unit (also a unit of weight) with a value which fluctuated, depending upon the particular monetary system which prevailed at a particular period of time. In Proverbs 23:23 it says, "buy to truth, and sell it not." The Bible describes two things that are truth, God's Word and God's Spirit. Just as we operate in a monetary system, heaven operates in a financial system. In the United States that system is the dollar, in heaven that system is the anointing.

God is showing us, who in the eyes of the world seem to be that servant with one talent, not to make this mistake. I pastor a little Church; I'm the door greeter; parking lot attendant; food bank; I think you get my point. God has given us the anointing, consider it of tremendous value and work for the Kingdom of God. There should not be one believer in the body of Christ that is not volunteering in the Church or in a community service.

In Matthew 10:29-30, " Are not two sparrows sold for

a copper coin? And not one of them falls to the ground apart from your Father's will. But the very hairs of your head are all numbered."

Talking about the little things here; not one sparrow falls to the ground with God's permission. Jesus says, God takes time to attend the sparrow's funeral. Jesus also points out that a hair is hard to notice, but God notices and each moment of one's life, He knows the count of our hair. The person who desires to operate in the anointing must view all things as God does. Luke says the same thing!

> *"Are not five sparrows sold for two copper coins?*
> *And not one of them is forgotten before God. But*
> *the very hairs of your head are all numbered.*
> *Do not fear therefore; you are of more value*
> *than many sparrows." Luke 12:6-7 NKJV*

There is a powerful teaching here on the anointing when we compare the two scriptures. Matthew says they sell two sparrows for a copper coin, but Luke says they sell five sparrows for two copper coins. The lesson is, when we are operating in the anointing God will throw in an extra sparrow. Two for one coin or 4 for two coins and the one extra is of no cost. When we due the things He anointed us for, God will always add. When I received the deliverance anointing and my eyes popped opened supernaturally, God has led me and added. This is how the "Exploring Secrets of the Heavenly Realms" series came into being. We must never forget God pays attention to detail, and everything has significance with God.

The anointing of the of God's Spirit is a must in the life of every believer. Every work done without the Spirit of God and without the power of God is rejected. The Bible labels work outside of the Holy Spirit dead works. Don't get religious here, truly think about this first. We must grasp God's infinite attention and His love for the works of His hands.

> *Now it is God who establishes and confirms us
> [in joint fellowship] with you in Christ, and who
> has anointed us [empowering us with the gifts
> of the Spirit]; 2 Corinthians 1:21 Amplified*

Coming full circle with what Paul tells the Corinthians. Paul says God is dependable to cause someone to be firm and established in belief through the gospel. The relationship or fellowship with God is through Christ Jesus and has anointed us and empowering us with gifts and talents through the working of the Holy Spirit. Think about what Jesus said in John 6 and how He feed the five thousand, gather the pieces and let nothing go to waste. This is God's attitude, let nothing be wasted.

Paul is revealing secrets to us concerning the anointing. He says, the presence of God is an abiding presence. This means we are to walk in fellowship or agreement with God. Anything outside of God's will and fellowship will interrupt the intimacy of that abiding presence. We know that God's will is His Word. The Apostle says, we are all anointed and the power of God is available to all who desire it and are willing to walk with God.

We also recognize the power of God comes for a reason. We must understand the season we are in and what we must learn in that season. There will be a presence for that season to encourage us, to make us established in the realities of that season. Always remember that in all things, nothing is to go to waste. Every success and every failure is the hand of God. Each through the process educating us in the supernatural and the Kingdom of Heaven. So every season will start with a seed principle. Think about what I am saying; develop patience and endurance, these are key in the anointing's growth. Like anything with God, both the presence and the anointing will grow as we walk with God.

CHAPTER SIX

FOCUSING ON GOD'S PRIORITIES PART 2

We have been talking about walking with God, which is the power of the anointing. This journey with God will require a radical change in our thinking. There is a Biblical word for change, and we call it repentance. We must repent for not having the power of the anointing because our ways and thoughts are not in line with God's. We see this clearly on Sunday morning in the Church. Most churches don't even come close to the early Church in the book of Acts. In previous chapters, we have discovered two objectives of God: His glory and satisfaction, and secondly His excellence. We concluded that God would not be glorified with anything else than excellence. We also see that excellence is the product of God's glory, and this is where the power of the anointing is visible; bringing God glory. So, if we are going to operate in the anointing, we must do it with the attitude of bringing God glory and meeting His satisfaction through excellence. Then we spoke about the two main priorities of God, His Kingdom come and His will be done, and secondly the eternal before the temporal. The anointing drives us to think about and care for the small things first, because in the small things an excellence is developed for success in the big things.

Now I want to talk about another perspective of God which is a vital key to the anointing, mercy and justice. Many people who desire the anointing cannot see these two things combined in God, yet it vividly displays the anointing as it flows. I was operating in the anointing in Sunday's prayer line. A woman experienced the fire of God, suddenly a piercing sharp pain hit her right side, I instantly knew the Holy Spirit was touching (mercy), but God wanted a demon cast out (justice). She hit the floor and began coughing up demons, then after the expulsion, the fire and shaking began again. Notice, God took the lead, and it was my job to walk with God in that prayer line. It was my assignment to aid in the physical what God was doing in the spiritual. I got down in her ear and coached the woman saying, cough out the demons, she instantly coughed. The Bible says that evil spirits are winds and that the believer must expel wind and fulfill the definition for freedom.

In Exodus 34 God descends in a cloud and proclaimed His name to Moses. We know from scripture that the name of God and or any person is a key to their nature.

> *Now the Lord descended in the cloud and stood*
> *with him there, and proclaimed the name of*
> *the Lord. And the Lord passed before him and*
> *proclaimed, "The Lord, the Lord God, merci-*
> *ful and gracious, longsuffering, and abound-*
> *ing in goodness and truth, keeping mercy for*
> *thousands, forgiving iniquity and transgression*
> *and sin, by no means clearing the guilty, visit-*
> *ing the iniquity of the fathers upon the children*
> *and the children's children to the third and the*
> *fourth generation." Exodus 34:5-7 NKJV*

In this passage of scripture, we can see without question God's two-sided nature. God Himself reveals to Moses a powerful revelation for all mankind to understand fully: God is first merciful, forgiving iniquity, transgression, and sin. Second, He is just, calling into account the guilty and allowing punishment to be generational, as it is with for-giveness.

I want to point out the seven aspects of His mercy as God listed them to Moses. God is merciful, gracious, long-suffering or patience, He abounds in goodness which the Bible can translate His steadfast love, abounds in truth which is also faithfulness, keeps mercy for thousands and last, God will forgive iniquity, transgression and sin. There they are, the seven aspects to God's mercy. But let none of us ever lose sight that this does not set aside God's judg-ment and His severity. The scripture reveals in the two last parts: He will not clear the guilty and He visits the iniquity of one generation on at least the following three generations.

These opposites run throughout the entire Bible, but some today can't see that. They believe that in the Old Testament God was terrible and dreadful, but in the New Testament He isn't. This is completely incorrect thinking. Does not Hebrews 13:8 say, Jesus Christ is the same yesterday, today, and forever.

For a believer to quote Ezekiel 18 here shows their ignorance of scripture and of God's name and nature. God is merciful, but He is also just. The word of the Lord came to me again, saying, what do you mean when you use this proverb concerning the land of Israel, saying: The fathers have eaten sour grapes, and the children's teeth are set on edge? God has pointed out to Ezekiel in the first two verses that the children are paying the price for the iniquities of their fathers. Then from verse three, God says they don't have to if they repent. Some have a hard time understanding that God does not change. We listen to these teachers that bring confusion to the scriptures because they can't manifest the power through the anointing.

Listen to what Ecclesiastes 9:8 says about the anointing and the two scriptures following and let me point out three things. We find the power anointing in the blood of Jesus, the reading of the scriptures and prayer. Here is something free, not mentioned in our three scriptures, we must exercise the anointing through encounter.

*Let your garments always be white,
and let your head lack no oil.*

*You prepare a table before me in the presence of my
enemies.
You have anointed and refreshed my head with oil;
My cup overflows Psalm 23:5 AMP*

*I counsel you to buy from Me gold that has
been heated red hot and refined by fire so that
you may become truly rich; and white clothes
[representing righteousness] to clothe yourself so that the shame of your nakedness will
not be seen; and healing salve to put on your
eyes so that you may see. Revelation 3:18*

We are talking about God's mercy and His severity or
justice. Today, most believers think the cross has covered
everything, and it has spiritually. In other words, spiritually we are saved, being saved, and going to be saved, 1 Peter
1. But as long as we are in this sinful body, experiencing
this sinful nature, this evil age has brought God's judgment upon mankind. Every student of the Bible can have
no other opinion if they are going to operate in the anointing. If death, sickness and tragedy can effect a Christian,
then the revelation of the New Testament is upon us, the
old man and the new man. I like to call this positional and
conditional Christianity. I have a book out on Amazon on
this subject called "The Mysterious Key to the New Testament: Secrets of the old man and new man."

Paul the Apostle speaks of the goodness and severity of God in Romans 11:22,

> *You will say then, "Branches were broken off that I might be grafted in." Well said. Because of unbelief they were broken off, and you stand by faith. Do not be haughty, but fear. For if God did not spare the natural branches, He may not spare you either. Therefore consider the goodness and severity of God: on those who fell, severity; but toward you, goodness, if you continue in His goodness. Otherwise you also will be cut off. Romans 11:19-22*

Here the Apostle is telling us that through unbelief God broke Israel off or to become detached from the whole. Israel had God but did not serve Him, so He broke off a part to graft in the Gentiles. But God changes not, and Paul warns the Roman believers to be on guard concerning God's goodness and severity. This becomes so clear as we operate in the anointing. Through the prophetic, healing, and deliverance anointing, God holds mankind accountable for the sins committed in this life, whether Christian or sinner. The difference between the two is the eternal place in which each one will live.

The definition for goodness here is the quality of being warmhearted, considerate, humane, gentle, and sympathetic; God is moral, righteous, and kind. This is the fruit of the anointing. Again, wc must never forget that God has two sides and if He has two sides, then there are two sides to the anointing. I have seen God not heal or deliver people because of sin, this is His judgment.

> *So wash and anoint yourself [with olive oil], then put on your [best] clothes, and go down to the threshing floor; but stay out of the man's sight until he has finished eating and drinking. Ruth 3:3 Amplified*

> *For the grace of God that brings salvation has appeared to all men, teaching us that, denying ungodliness and worldly lusts, we should live soberly, righteously, and godly in the present age, looking for the blessed hope and glorious appearing of our great God and Savior Jesus Christ, who gave Himself for us, that He might redeem us from every lawless deed and purify for Himself His own special people, zealous for good works. Titus 2:11-14 NKJV*

We surely can see in these two scriptures how living a righteous and moral life affects the anointing. The atmosphere within will produce an atmosphere outwardly that shifts our sphere of operation. This is the anointing! We live a lifestyle of washing and moral character as Ruth tells us. Titus is saying, live in a way that salvation (sanctification) teaches us to deny ungodliness and worldly lusts.

> *But the anointing which you have received from Him abides in you, and you do not need that anyone teach you; but as the same anointing teaches you concerning all things, and is true,*

*and is not a lie, and just as it has taught you,
you will abide in Him. 1 John 2:27 NKJV*

The Apostle John here describes two different realms to the anointing. I have felt the false anointing before! The false anointing feels supernatural but, adultery, fornication, uncleanness, lewdness, idolatry, sorcery, hatred, contentions, jealousies, outbursts of wrath, selfish ambitions, dissensions, heresies, envy, murders, drunkenness, revelries, and the like; This is what the false anointing feels like and the fruits of its manifestation. The true anointing of the Holy Spirit feels like love, joy, peace, longsuffering, kindness, goodness, faithfulness, gentleness, self-control. Therefore, the origin of each anointing originates in nature, character, and fruit of the supernatural being. My point, if the Holy Spirit manifests in fruit and power, we to must walk with Him in this type of character. A pure heart does not need to be totally pure, God looks at the desire and response of the heart.

When we live aware of the Spirit of God in us, we are much more prone to realize when His anointing is released from us. The faith, character, and nature of the believer is closely linked to the power of the anointing. We must comprehend that power is released in greater measures through understanding. We cannot operate in a realm effectively if we do not understand it.

There are many, if not all, power ministries that operate in the goodness of God, yet lack the scriptural knowledge of the severity of God for operating in the anointing. Somewhere along the way, ministries have allowed the kingdom of darkness to take away this side of God's nature. God loves beyond our understanding, but He is also just. Is it hard to give a prophetic word that calls for a change in an edifying way, no! Just like it is easy to explain to people that sin will keep them from their healing or deliverance. The prophet Micah shows us the justice of God to a covenant people,

> *Therefore I will also make you sick by striking you,*
> *By making you desolate because of your sins.*
> *Micah 6:13 NKJV*

I have had many ministry sessions that behavior has caused the power of God not to operate. Here is one that I have never forgotten, the curse of not tithing.

> *Will a man rob God? Yet you have robbed Me! But*
> *you say,*
> *'In what way have we robbed You?'*
> *In tithes and offerings. You are cursed with a curse,*
> *For you have robbed Me, Even this whole nation.*
> *Malachi 3:8-9 NKJV*

I have a saying based on a ministry session that revealed to all the goodness and severity of God in a matter in two minutes or less. A lady was manifesting demons as I was preaching the gospel. She was manifesting in the meeting, so she had to be escorted out of the room, but when the time came to deal with the issues, the demons would not manifest. God spoke and said, "She is not a tither, so a curse is upon her." I led her through repentance and the breaking of the curse. She was very poor. God told me to have her tithe her monthly grocery bill. She put twelve dollars in the offering basket and immediately twelve demons left her. Once the woman obeyed the Word of God, His severity ended and His goodness came in power. I have thousands of stories like this one. The saying is, and I'm joking, but it appears God has put a price tag on demons, a dollar a demon.

I will sing of the mercies of the Lord forever;
With my mouth will I make known Your faithful-
ness to all generations.
For I have said, "Mercy shall be built up forever;
Your faithfulness You shall establish in the very
heavens."
Psalm 89:1 NKJV

We can sing of the mercies of God forever or we can proclaim to all mankind God's goodness, but we can never forget that there is another side to God. This is the power of the anointing! The anointing makes people aware of divine moments, and these periods will come through the anointing in God's goodness or His severity. For some reason this is hard for the New Testament believer. We are taught from the Church to focus on the goodness of God. We also see believers coming out of these supernatural schools trained to operate out of God's goodness, but not out of His justice. Many times I have desired to bring fire and healing, but end up in an exorcism. The anointing does not serve me, but I serve the anointing. Again, if we are truthful, we notice these two realities run throughout the entire Bible.

> *Tell and bring forth your case; Yes, let them take counsel together. Who has declared this from ancient time? Who has told it from that time? Have not I, the Lord? And there is no other God besides Me, A just God and a Savior; There is none besides Me. Isaiah 45:21 NKJV*

We see Isaiah showing the two aspects of God, He is just and a Savior or merciful. Everyone of us is going to have to related to these principles of God. He is willing to save and show mercy, but He will execute justice on all. Paul speaks of this very thing,

> *But if our unrighteousness demonstrates the righteousness of God, what shall we say? God is not wrong to inflict His wrath [on us], is He? (I am speaking in purely human terms.) Certainly not! For otherwise, how will God judge the world? Romans 3:5-6 AMP*

Paul knows what they are thinking, "If my sinfulness makes God look so good, then why should he punish me? I'm actually helping him out!" This was an attempt to make it seem unfair for God to punish sinners. Many believe that God's wrath contradicts his loving nature. But God judges based on His own character, not on society's norm for fairness. God is not accountable to some external, vague notion of fair play. His personal moral uprightness is the standard by which he judges.

This reality I have found true, the anointing of God first wants man to repent, but in no terms will God leave the guilty unpunished. God seeks to establish truth, and He does it through His Word and His power. God's goodness and kindness is beyond comprehension and He desires us to get caught up with whom He is and what He is doing. This is the power of the anointing! Those that operate out of the goodness of God only will never fulfill their destiny to the fullest. Here is another hard saying, but it does not make it less true. These people coming out of supernatural schools are moving in the power, but most are full of demons. The anointing wants to bring justice!

The reason I'm writing about this subject in this chapter is because God expects us to have the same attitude He does. In, Psalm 97:10 the scripture uses two words: love and hate. Are not these two words very strong? We can say, those who operate in the anointing will love the Lord with all their heart, but it will compel us to deal with the kingdom of darkness; hating what God hates. The palmist reveals a corresponding attitude here, loving the Lord and hating evil. This is the power of the anointing! I am compelled to bring Kingdom power and glory to God, but I'm driven to cast out demons; loving God and hating evil! These are the two sides of the power anointing. We must allow the anointing to develop the same two characteristic of God in us. Therefore, if we love the Lord we will not compromise with evil. To compromise with evil through the anointing is not to cast out evil spirits. We must operate in Kingdom power by healing the sick and cast out evil spirits. Therefore, let us not be inconsistent and let us deal with evil also!

We never assume that God's mercy sets aside His judgment. So many people make that mistake today. Christian theologians, ministers and others weaken their anointing and calling by not dealing with God's severity. Again, many times I will shift into corporate deliverance or in the prayer line move in deliverance, this is the power of the anointing moving against the kingdom of darkness. The anointing demands justice on behalf of the believer. At times, the anointing will treat evil spirits harshly. The evil spirit will be compelled by the anointing to come out or given reason for possession. This too is the power of the anointing!

Listen to what 2 Peter 3:6-10 says,

> *by which the world that then existed perished, being flooded with water. But the heavens and the earth which are now preserved by the same word, are reserved for fire until the day of judgment and perdition of ungodly men.*

> *But, beloved, do not forget this one thing, that with the Lord one day is as a thousand years, and a thousand years as one day. The Lord is not slack concerning His promise, as some count slackness, but is longsuffering toward us, not willing that any should perish but that all should come to repentance.*

Peter is speaking about God's judgments on the world. He speaks about the flood by water; God destroyed the world of that time. Peter says, by the same word, the present heavens are reserved for fire and of a judgment of ungodly men. There is a day of judgment! The Lord says the very thing to Peter that He said to Moses: the Lord is patience not wanting anyone to perish but all come to Him in repentance. There it is God's goodness and His severity. We do not get to say, God treats the sin of the believer differently than that of the unbeliever. God's patience will not set aside His judgment on wickedness. Again, the difference between the believer and the unbeliever is their eternal destination. We do not talk about this side of the anointing very much. It surely is not taught in the Church. If God anoints us with His power, then we understand that it is for His goodness and severity! When we look a little further in 2 Peter 3, he says, make ever effort to be found spotless, blameless and at peace with Him. Peter is openly warning the believers! This is the power of the anointing, calling the Church to holiness. The anointing will manifest God's goodness and His severity on evil.

The anointing teaches us salvation for those who meet His conditions, but it does not set aside the judgment for those who reject God's mercy. Let me say this as I seek to close the chapter, most believers never allow God to bring judgment on the kingdom of darkness, because most do not go through deliverance and then exorcism. Is not Peter warning Christians? He says, because God's judgment seems to be delayed don't imagine He has cancelled it. We fully understand the principle that God is manifesting His power. We all must take this time and be reconciled with God through sanctification before the judgment comes. God has given the power anointing to heal the sick and the authority anointing to drive out evil spirits.

Let us look at the wrong attitude in man, in Ecclesiastes 8:11, "because the sentence against an evil work is not executed speedily, therefore the heart of the sons of men is fully set in them to do evil."

Because we don't yield to both sides of the anointing and see His judgment on evil spirits immediately, people think God will not judge them and they think it safe to do evil. It is the anointing that destroys's strongholds such as these. Remember, we are talking about walking with God, the power of the anointing!

Chapter Seven

Thinking In Categories

We have just covered a very difficult subject on the anointing, and the two sides the anointing operates out of God's goodness and severity. I have been writing about the four main areas in which the anointing thrives. Also, if we intend to operate in the anointing, we must agree with God; our thoughts and ways must be His thoughts and ways. The secret to the anointing is to walk with God in His objectives, His priorities, His attitudes and His categories. In these four subjects, we must bring our thoughts and ways in line with God's ways and thoughts. I want to reiterate something of vital importance; the one who desires to operate in the anointing must seek to walk with God.

Last night in our prayer meeting, God's Spirit was very thick and most of the people were shaking and travailing, others felt like fire was upon them. As the prayer meeting came to a close, and we soaked in His presence, the power of God's anointing had made a woman feel sick to her stomach, suddenly she began coughing out demons. As pastor of Church In One Accord, it is my job to walk with God and follow the leading of the Holy Spirit. The prayer group thanked the Lord for setting His daughter free. After God's Spirit had His way, holy laughter broke out. It was my responsibility to make sure the place was conducive for deliverance. If it had not, the appropriate action would have been to have some ladies take the woman to a private place, but not shut down the deliverance. I am to walk with God, not stand in disagreement with Him.

We have read in earlier chapters about the two main objectives I believe that is of most importance: first God's own glory and satisfaction, second His excellence. We found out that excellence is needed for God's glory and satisfaction. The ultimate purpose of everything is to bring glory to God and to satisfy God. There is no higher call and no other purpose for the anointing. We have learned the two primary priorities of God: the first is the coming of God's Kingdom to earth and second is the eternal before the temporal. God will never sacrifice the eternal for the temporal. God always works in our lives for our eternal good. Then I wrote about two characteristic attitudes of God, first His attention to detail. It always concerns Him about the small before the great. If we are faithful in the little, we will be faithful in much. Second is God's mercy and severity. These things must be in the heart of those who seek to operate in the anointing. We know that to apply oil or to receive the anointing is part of a religious rite that consecrates someone or something to God.

Now I will move on to the fourth primary area, that of categories. Categories is a way we classify things or grouping them together. What I am talking about is the way we categorize things or persons has a tremendous influence on how we relate to them and how we deal with them. I have seen so many Christians reject the power of God because it did not fit their perspective or viewpoint. We have this fallen nature that wants to be a god by categorizing things negatively or positively. I like to quote the Apostle Paul and say, let God be true and every man a liar, Romans 3:4. How do we commonly categorize people? The person is a baptist, evangelist, prophet, deliverance minister or different political party or ethnic group. How we relate to that person can or will not set up barriers. I like to move in the fire of God, see healing take place, and cast out demons; I also like to do this in corporate settings. If we view these things hastily, we establish barriers and miss out on the power of God.

God has used two powerful ministers to pass on the anointing: the first was Benny Hinn, and the second was Bob Larson. How people view these two ministries is what measure they can receive from them. Both are completely legit ministries and the Holy Spirit has supernaturally witnessed to the authenticity of these two ministries through the transference of the anointing and instantly operating in that anointing. Second has been through supernatural encounter where the Holy Spirit Himself has taken over and performed signs and wonders through a series of events during a ministry session. How I categorized those two ministries negatively or positively was a direct connection to whether I received the anointing. It also would have a lasting impact on whether I would fulfill my destiny. It was the will of God that I received the transference of God's anointing through those two ministries. If I had rejected in any way what they were moving in, I would not have written the series called, "Exploring Secrets of the Heavenly Realms." I also probably would not be writing this book on how to walk with God, the power of the anointing. Therefore, our view of people or the things of the spirit realm has a direct impact on our anointing, the levels of operation of the anointing and also the destiny of our walking with God.

After the Touch

Once the anointing came, I was instantly invited into realms of the Holy Spirit that required intense Bible study and prayer. It became my responsibility to learn the ways of God and how He thinks. Let us be real here. This is an impossible task! But what I have learned is to follow the power of God and so letting Him pick the time and place. The simple formula is to seek God's presence and allow the manifestations. God has required me to study Him through His Word and be on guard for the counterfeit. I have been around the power of both kingdoms, the Kingdom of God and the kingdom of evil, both seem to manifest when I step into the spirit world. I'm looking to bring God glory and I am also looking to destroy the works of darkness. I love when the fire falls, when healing breaks out, and I love to see the anointing defeat God's enemies.

We are talking about relating to the things of the spirit and how it determines our attitude. The conclusion then is the way we categorize people or things determines our attitude toward them and how we relate and receive from them. Therefore, if we are to walk with God in the anointing's power, we must learn to think in God's categories. It requires a forcible overthrow of any belief system we may have that does not line up with the way God does things. I realize that most believers are not even aware of this revelation. By rejecting a function of the Holy Spirit is to reject God Himself and the anointing will not touch our life.

With God, the most important categories are spiritual and moral. Let us look at a spiritual category or what we will label moving forward, a spiritual reality. The spiritual reality here has great importance to God. The basic spiritual reality or the foundational spiritual reality in all of scripture is faith or unbelief. Let us look at these two realities or categories from scripture in John 3:18 NKJV,

> *He who believes in Him is not condemned; but he who does not believe is condemned already, because he has not believed in the name of the only begotten Son of God.*

There it is, the one who believes and the one who does not believe. We are looking at the basic reality and how God groups people. The word condemned is a strong word; It means to judge a person to be guilty and liable to punishment. Because God looks at both the eternal and the temporal, how does believing or not believing affect us. Could there be areas in our life that unbelief still holds us captive or guilty? It is the power of the anointing that brings invisible realities forward for mankind to agree with God or not. Earlier in the chapter, I said that we are not to shut down God's power but to agree; This is walking with God through the power of the anointing. John says, when we do not believe it brings us under condemnation. I know some don't like things like this, but if we operate in the anointing long enough, we see it is true.

> *He who believes and trusts in the Son and accepts Him [as Savior] has eternal life [that is, already possesses it]; but he who does not believe the Son and chooses to reject Him, [disobeying Him and denying Him as Savior] will not see [eternal] life, but [instead] the wrath of God hangs over him continually." John 3:36 AMP*

There again we have two simple basic categories, he who believes and has everlasting life and he who does not believe who is under the wrath of God. This applies not only in the person of Jesus but in the gospel's message. Those that operate in the anointing understands fully, the anointing compels us to believe in the Son of God, His message and a desire to fulfill it.

When Jesus commissioned the apostles to go forth at the end of Mark's gospel, with the gospel message to all creation, He told them this:

> *And He said to them, "Go into all the world and preach the gospel to every creature. He who believes and is baptized will be saved; but he who does not believe will be condemned. Mark 16:15-16 NKJV*

We see the two sides or the dividing line, those that believe and those that don't believe. We can see the goal here, not to build a big Church or to get many to say the salvation prayer, but to build people through their conversion to the gospel's message. Once people believe the message and are adhering to it, then this is what the anointing will do:

> *And these signs will follow those who believe: In My name they will cast out demons; they will speak with new tongues; they will take up serpents; and if they drink anything deadly, it will by no means hurt them; they will lay hands on the sick, and they will recover." Mark 16:17-18 NKJV*

There is no substitute for the anointing! God's anointing upon a believer makes an impact as that one prays in the Holy Spirit or with their prayer language. The anointing will cause demons to react and come out of believers. When we pray for the sick, we will see people healed. The anointing will cause the believer who is trained in each of these categories to have success and to bring glory to God.

The Anointing and Culture

I have been sharing throughout this book things that God values and it is our assignment through the anointing to discover and implement them. Without an understanding of how God places importance, we cannot fully realize God's purposes in the earth. Walking with God is a continual transformation of how heaven operates and how to apply it on earth.

Walking with God through the power of the anointing will bring an instant change in our lives, in those around us, and in the culture we seek to establish. The believer who allows the Holy Spirit to mentor them will experience new and fresh things of the spirit realm. The Holy Spirit will always cause us to see that there is more than what someone has expressed today. What do I mean by this? When the anointing leads us into a dimension we know nothing about, God's Spirit seeks to empower us. It was God's purpose for my life to discover and secrets of the kingdom of darkness and the multi-level empire that operates against God and His people. The function of the anointing as we walk with God is to bring to a close this age. Each one of us must fulfill their calling as we walk with God.

The Oxford Dictionary's definition of empower is to give (someone) the authority or power to do something; make (someone) stronger and more confident. What is given, the anointing! How does the anointing bring out authority through training! The anointing moves through understanding and reveals the operation of the spirit realm? The centurion in Matthew 8 understood, the power of his government was behind him as long as he did his job lawfully. This is what the anointing does as we walk with God. The anointing will through the Bible and spiritual encounters teach us the laws of God and how to exercise those laws. What we now understand is, the laws of God bring authority and the anointing is the power of God to exercise those laws.

Again, if we intend to operate in the anointing, we must agree with God; our thoughts and ways must be His thoughts and ways. The secret to the anointing is to walk with God in His objectives, His priorities, His attitudes and His categories. Now let us look at a very simple but practical way of daily life, marriage, concerning belief and unbelief.

Do not be unequally yoked together with unbelievers. For what fellowship has righteousness with lawlessness? And what communion has light with darkness? And what accord has Christ with Belial? Or what part has a believer with an unbeliever? And what agreement has the temple of God with idols? For you are the temple of the living God. As God has said:

> *"I will dwell in them*
> *And walk among them.*
> *I will be their God,*
> *And they shall be My people."*
> *2 Corinthians 6:14-16*

The scriptures throughout continues to reveal the same basic classification of the believer and the unbeliever. I want to reiterate something of vital importance; the one who desires to operate in the anointing must seek to walk with God. Belial is another name used in the Bible for Satan and is actually a name for one of the fallen angels. For more on fallen angels read my book series, "Exploring Secrets of the Heavenly Realms." So, when we choose a spouse, this is the basic issue, do they believe in Christ Jesus and are they willing to carry out through the power of the Holy Spirit the message.

When God anointed me, the great influencer, the Holy Spirit came upon me and inspires me to do what I never thought I could do. This is the power of the anointing! The anointing will lead us into the impossible and will make up the difference so we can understand what is being presented. From hospital beds to fallen angels, it has always been the Holy Spirit who has revealed the unknown and the hunger to pursue to achieve a purpose.

One thing I've learned about the anointing, it is attractive, and it draws people. People seek to be included so they can grow in their gifts and make a difference in the world. Another powerful thing about the anointing is that it draws apprentices. They first want what you have, but it is the one who will pay the price that receives. In other words, they will have to walk with God down the same paths you walked to receive the anointing, and all it accomplishes. This is what the writer of Proverbs 23:23 was speaking of when he states, "Buy the truth, and sell it not."

CHAPTER SEVEN

The anointing is priceless!

Another principle of the anointing I have found invaluable, it is the privilege and our responsibility to pass on what we have learned and the realm we have attained to the next generation. It is our calling to train and equip those who have received the anointing so they may empower others. The anointing will create an empowering culture, and the anointing I walk in is to be given to those who have paid the same price I have.

The principle I want to draw out concerning 2 Corinthians 6:14-16 is, if we think in terms of God's categories we can refrain from marrying someone who doesn't have the desire to go into the world and preach the gospel, with signs and wonders following. Therefore, faith centers in the will of man, not in the intellect. Faith is a decision, and those decisions will have a direct impact on the anointing. We can decide to think in God's categories, faith or unbelief.

In Hebrews 10:35-39, it gives us a very solemn or serious warning. If you look at this scripture closely, there are only two possibilities, we go on to believing and in the power of the Holy Spirit or we shrink back to destruction. Hebrews encourages us to go on to our full salvation, yet the writer says, the choice will come. This is so powerful! I see many who are anointed not attain the highest call of their anointing. The Holy Spirit told me years ago, if I continue in what I know, I will be out of date in 10 years. I have also witnessed some who have given up and shrink back, no longer pursuing the power of God. They sit in powerless churches and go through the same program every Sunday.

Before we move on to our next category, I want us to think about how Jesus only taught, equipped, and anointed twelve, yet He ministered to thousands. Therefore, very few will have the heart to see what God's vast anointing can do. Some will purse healing and never get involved in deliverance. Some will follow the prophetic, but give no account to the healing anointing. I think you get my point. If we have been anointed, it is the Holy Spirit and His knowledge and power that operates the gifts, all nine. The true anointing will never be one- or two-dimensional.

THINKING IN GOD'S MORALITY

When my steps were bathed with cream, and the rock poured out rivers of oil for me! Job 29:6 NKJV

There are direct repercussions on our moral state for the anointing. Job says, when I followed the word of God it cleansed me and God poured out His Spirit on me like a river. The cream represents the wealth of God's Word and how the power of the anointing flows, like a river.

Cream is produced by the centrifugal separation of milk. During separation, it creates two streams, a highly concentrated milk fat stream termed cream and a non-fat stream of skim milk that can be further processed into evaporated or dried milk products. Therefore, the anointing is the highly concentrated power of God that flows like a river. The believer who does not seek and or develop the anointing is like a nonfat or powerless stream whose works evaporate. The word centrifugal is to move away from a center, that is, when we move away from walking with God, it has great effects on our state of being and the operation of the anointing.

Then a spirit passed before my face; the
hair on my body stood up. It stood still, but
I could not discern its appearance. A form
was before my eyes; there was silence; then I
heard a voice saying: Job 4:15-16 NKJV

Job tells us that an image was before his eyes. Job was in a vision. The presence of God made his hair on his body stand up. Job saw the vision in his mind, then heard the voice through his thoughts. When we are silent before the presence of God, those mental areas come forward and the knowing in the heart takes place. This is the power of the anointing, the ability to sit silent before God in His presence. This can only happen as we are walking with God in morality.

As we come to the end of this section of the book, I have been writing about agreeing with God in our thinking. The power of the anointing is to identify with God's thinking in four main areas. The four areas I have suggested are objectives, priorities, attitudes and categories. We must bring our thinking in every one of those areas in line with God to see the full power of the anointing. We have to share or partner with God's objectives, His priorities, His attitudes, and God's categories.

We just discussed in this chapter the way we categorize things or persons determines in a large measure how we relate to them. This is so important in operating in the anointing. I can't tell you how many times I have looked or thought things about a person, and the power of God does the exact opposite. For instance, someone received their healing when I thought it would not happen. I categorized that individual but the power of the anointing caused me to look at it a different way. So, categorization might separate me from someone or draw me to someone.

In scripture, it reveals the way God categorizes people. And it is extremely important that we understand for the power of the anointing to move. The primary spiritual category revealed in scripture is faith or unbelief. For the anointing to flow, does that individual believe or does he not believe?

Let us look at God's moral categories when seeking to operate in the anointing. Let us go to 1 John, which is as clear and as thorough an example of these categories as we can find anywhere in the Bible. One of the main themes in this epistle is to unfold God's categories to us. We will notice in every case they are clear cut opposites. This is what the anointing does; It separates what God approves and what God does not approve. There is hardly any room for compromise!

This is the message which we have heard from

Him and declare to you, that God is light and
in Him is no darkness at all. 1 John 1:5 NKJV

Notice it is a clear-cut opposition when speaking of God's person. Then John goes on in the very next verse to say,

If we say that we have fellowship with Him,
and walk in darkness, we lie and do not
practice the truth. 1 John 1:6 NKJV

Notice again the clear-cut opposites! These things affect how the anointing operates. To walk with God and operate in the anointing's power, we must agree or have fellowship with God. The definition of fellowship here is to participate through a close association: the act of sharing in the activities or privileges of an intimate and mutual interest.

All the way through this epistle John distinguishes between sin and righteousness. Then in the second chapter of the epistle of John,

He who says he is in the light, and hates his broth-
er, is in darkness until now. He who loves his
brother abides in the light, and there is no cause
for stumbling in him. 1 John 2:9-10 NKJV

Notice the clear-cut opposites here, hate or love, and John implies that there is not much in-between. Let me suggest something very powerful here and that is, if we don't love it will descend into hate. This is a powerful truth when operating in the anointing.

> *Do not love the world or the things in the world. If anyone loves the world, the love of the Father is not in him. For all that is in the world—the lust of the flesh, the lust of the eyes, and the pride of life—is not of the Father but is of the world. 1 John 2:15-16 NKJV*

Here John is focusing on what we love! This will increase or reduce the anointing we operate in. John points out two mutually exclusive objects of love. If we love the Father, we will not love this present world order. If we love this present world order, then we cannot love the Father; they are mutually exclusive. Therefore, everyone of those pairs of opposites we have looked at are mutually exclusive and is characteristic of God's moral categories.

I want to continue with just a few more mutually exclusive pairs of opposites that will have a great impact on the anointing.

> *He who sins is of the devil, for the devil has sinned from the beginning. For this purpose the Son of God was manifested, that He might destroy the works of the devil. Whoever has been born of God does not sin, for His seed remains in him; and he cannot sin, because he has been born of God. 1 John 3:8-9 NKJV*

John points out two alternative sources of influence and authority, even direction in our lives. John suggests that there is no third opposition. It is of God or the devil. This is not the way people think today, and so are ineffective in operating in the anointing. We are talking about God's categories! We cannot walk with God in the anointing's power if we cannot think like God.

> *We know that we have passed from death to life, because we love the brethren. He who does not love his brother abides in death. 1 John 3:14 NKJV*

Here is another clear-cut issue, death or life. To love the brethren is to be in life or do not love the brethren is to be in death. There is no other opposition. Again, this is a category that will have a direct impact on the anointing.

> *My little children, let us not love in word or in tongue, but in deed and in truth. 1 John 3:18 NKJV*

Here we have two pairs of opposites. Love on the one hand that is in word or tongue, superficial or love that is in deed and in truth. We say we love and prove it by our action or we say we love and deny it by our actions. The anointing is always trying to tackle these categories so we can make an impact. We should question the experience of anyone who says he has encountered the anointing, but is not willing to undergo the process within these categories. In fact, it is a great privilege to be invited into this transformation so that the anointing will grow. The anointing's power is measured by our love for people and in the way we serve them.

> *Love has been perfected among us in this: that we may have boldness in the day of judgment; because as He is, so are we in this world. There is no fear in love; but perfect love casts out fear, because fear involves torment. But he who fears has not been made perfect in love. 1 John 4:17-18 NKJV*

The two opposites here are fear and boldness. If we do not develop boldness, we are subject to fear, and that will block the anointing. We have covered just some of God's moral categories and their opposites that the believer must develop to operate in the anointing's power.

I must bring out one more point before closing this chapter. It is on these bases, the bases of these opposites, we will face the judgment of God. It is also true, on these bases of opposites we will bring the judgment of God, His justice or severity. This is how the anointing will grow and impact nations. We find this in 2 Corinthians 5:10.

Chapter Eight

The Holy Spirit and the Anointing

The person and the work of the Holy Spirit is one of the most profound and distinctive revelations of the whole Bible. Through it we receive a kind of knowledge we could not receive in any other way. One of the supremely important revelations of the Bible is the nature of God. The Bible unfolds a mystery we could never know through any other source. The mystery is, God is both one and yet more than one. God is three persons, yet one God. The three persons revealed in scripture are the Father, the Son, and the Holy Spirit.

In this book, we have been dealing with the Holy Spirit and the anointing's power. The first thing we need to understand is that the Holy Spirit is Himself a person, and the anointing is the power of that person. The Holy Spirit is a person just as much as the Father and the Son. When the Spirit of the Lord comes upon us, it is He that brings the anointing. Second, the anointing is always for a reason. Third, we move in the power of the Holy Spirit. Fourth, we know that He anoints us.

Through, the Holy Spirit God is omniscient and omnipresent. Therefore, God is all-knowing, all-wise and all-seeing. God is also present everywhere in the universe at the same time. We could say that the creation is sustained by God's person. God in the person of His Spirit is not only everywhere, all-knowing but also all-powerful or omnipotent. The Bible calls these three attributes the anointing. The anointing seeks to empower the believer in knowledge, power, and to expand the sphere of the human spirit.

> *"Am I a God near at hand," says the Lord,*
> *"And not a God afar off?*
> *Can anyone hide himself in secret places,*
> *So I shall not see him?" says the Lord;*
> *"Do I not fill heaven and earth?" says the Lord.*
> *Jeremiah 23:23-24 NKJV*

What does it mean to fill heaven and earth? The definition is to fill up, be full, i.e., have a quantity of space filled with a mass or collection in a container or contained area. What the Holy Spirit is telling Jeremiah, God's Spirit not only contains heaven and earth, but He is even larger than heaven and earth. God is also near or not far in distance, time, space, degree, or circumstances. God is always nearby everyone. There is no place where God is not. There is no place that things happen that God does not know about. This is unfolded more in Psalms 139:1-12 NKJV,

O Lord, You have searched me and known me.
You know my sitting down and my rising up;
You understand my thought afar off.
You comprehend my path and my lying down,
And are acquainted with all my ways.
For there is not a word on my tongue,
But behold, O Lord, You know it altogether.
You have hedged me behind and before,
And laid Your hand upon me.
Such knowledge is too wonderful for me;
It is high, I cannot attain it.
Where can I go from Your Spirit?
Or where can I flee from Your presence?
If I ascend into heaven, You are there;
If I make my bed in hell, behold, You are there.
If I take the wings of the morning,
And dwell in the uttermost parts of the sea,
Even there Your hand shall lead me,
And Your right hand shall hold me.
If I say, "Surely the darkness shall fall on me,"
Even the night shall be light about me;
Indeed, the darkness shall not hide from You,
But the night shines as the day;
The darkness and the light are both alike to You.

Notice the powerful revealing of God's greatness and His wisdom. The fact is, God's presence permeates our universe. There is nowhere we can go from God and be hidden from Him. It should comfort us that no distance or circumstance can separate us from God's Spirit. There is no darkness that can hide us from Him. There is no evil power that can hold us from God when we call out to Him; God is everywhere throughout the entire universe. I believe we find the key to these scriptures in the seventh verse. God's Spirit or His presence, that is His person is everywhere. If the Holy Spirit is everywhere, then His power is also everywhere. The anointing can touch people all over the world from any location. The definition of the anointing means to rub on or to paint. When something is rubbed on or painted on, it becomes one with the object. Just as God's Spirit is one with Him, so the anointing desires to become one with us. This is the anointing's power!

The Holy Spirit has been active in the creation from the very beginning.

By the word of the Lord the heavens were made,
And all the host of them by the breath of His
mouth.
Psalm 33:6 NKJV

The Hebrew says spirit and not breath. God's word and His Spirit made the heavens. We also see something not talked about much, all the hosts. Here the Bible is talking about the angels. What we also discover is multiple heavens. The two great agents of creation that brought the universe into being were the word of the Lord and the Spirit of the Lord. Therefore, the anointing becomes part of us and in a sense belongs to us as we walk in those things we are anointed to do.

> *To console those who mourn in Zion,*
> *To give them beauty for ashes,*
> *The oil of joy for mourning,*
> *The garment of praise for the spirit of heaviness;*
> *That they may be called trees of righteousness,*
> *The planting of the Lord, that He may be glorified.*
> *Isaiah 61:3 NKJV*

The anointing is the joy for those in deep sorrow or grief. The anointing is the praise when the garment or mantle is applied against the spirit of heaviness or depression. The goal of the anointing is to make strong believers that live righteously. It would plant us for God's glory.

The point I am trying to make is that God is everywhere and He can do anything, yet He desires us to participate with Him in managing His creation. In the Genesis account, the word and the Spirit were present and the light came. The result was that everything God did was good. This too is the function of the anointing, to bring light so mankind can see the goodness of God.

When we study the anointing of the Holy Spirit in the Old Testament, we see it was the Holy Spirit who inspired and empowered all those God used. The list is too long to give all the names. But when we are anointed it will manifest itself. However, there are dangers to the anointing. Besides sin, the biggest danger is to be so caught up in doing the Lord's work we forget the disciplines that empower the anointing.

Like Samson, the anointing can slip away, and we will hardly realize it. You can feel this! It is likened to operating in the anointing not so intensified. Let me say it this way: the anointing was lightweight in feeling and had lost its quality or attractiveness and needed to be put back or renewed.

DEEP DISCOVERIES

One function of the anointing is to discover what is in the heart of God for His people. It is through encounter that God reveals those secrets.

> *For God has unveiled them and revealed them to us through the [Holy] Spirit; for the Spirit searches all things [diligently], even [sounding and measuring] the [profound] depths of God [the divine counsels and things far beyond human understanding]. 1 Corinthians 2:10 AMPB*

Within this scripture we can see God's knowledge, His power through His works, and His omnipresence. This scripture also alludes to man being created in God's likeness. We see this likeness made for the purpose of companionship. Through intimacy God's Spirit searches for us our purpose and destiny. Therefore, the anointing takes what God reveals, our calling, purpose, and destiny, and drives us to the eternal.

CHAPTER EIGHT

Now Joshua the son of Nun was filled with the spirit of wisdom, for Moses had laid his hands on him; so the sons of Israel listened to him and did as the Lord commanded Moses. Deuteronomy 34:9

Moses laid his hands on Joshua and the spirit of wisdom filled him. There are seven touches of the Holy Spirit, Spirit of the Lord, and the Spirits of wisdom, of understanding, of counsel, of might, of knowledge and of fear of the LORD. This is what the anointing seeks to accomplish. God has given to no other part of creation the anointing to access these realms. Joshua became a great military leader because God filled him with the Spirit. Empowering leaders is what the anointing seeks to do. It will also give leaders faith to empower people under their leadership.

The Father's plan from the beginning was to empower mankind so we would become world changers. The Holy Spirit who raised Jesus from the dead lives in us. It was the person of the Holy Spirit that commanded the resurrection, but it was the anointing of the Holy Spirit or the power of the Holy Spirit that accomplished it. The Spirit-filled believer has the anointing dwelling within and it is to flow out of us, touching everyone around us. In Judges 6:34, the Spirit of the Lord came upon Gideon and made him the mighty leader he was. Before God's Spirit touched him, he was a timid man cowering at the winepress, but the Spirit of God changed him, but it was the anointing that caused him to blow the trumpet.

The very same thing happened to David! In 2 Samuel 23:1-2, David tells us how he gave us those beautiful psalms, the Spirit of the Lord spoke to me, because God's word was on his tongue. That prophetic anointing would come upon David and he would speak the word of God by the Spirit of God. Those listed in Hebrews 11 all learned to walk with God so the anointing's power could flow. It is not enough to be anointed, the impact of the anointing is when we walk with God. They learned to serve God acceptably and effectively doing so through the power of the Holy Spirit. The anointing's power did completely the works of the Old Testament saints.

We have read in earlier chapters about the two main objectives I believe are of most importance: first God's own glory and satisfaction, and second His excellence. We found out that excellence is needed for God's glory and satisfaction. The ultimate purpose of everything is to bring glory to God and to satisfy God. There is no higher call and no other purpose for the anointing. We have learned the two primary priorities of God: the first is the coming of God's Kingdom to earth and second is the eternal before the temporal. God will never sacrifice the eternal for the temporal. God always works in our lives for our eternal good. Then I wrote about two characteristic attitudes of God, first His attention to detail. It always concerns Him about the small before the great. If we are faithful in the little, we will be faithful in much. Second is God's mercy and severity. These things must be in the heart of those who seek to operate in the anointing. Then we discussed the fourth primary area, that of categories. Categories is a way we classify things or grouping them together. When we can understand why God anoints and for what purposes, then we can properly move into proper function and destiny through the anointing.

FIRE OF THE ANOINTING

John the Baptist, who came specifically to reveal Jesus and prepare the way for His ministry, introduced Him under one particular title, "the Baptizer in the Holy Spirit." It was John's calling and anointing to make Jesus known by name to the people of Israel. John provided an opening explanation or announcement in Matthew 3:11.

> *"As for me, I baptize you with water for repentance, but He who is coming after me is mightier than I, and I am not fit to remove His sandals; He will baptize you with the Holy Spirit and fire. Matthew 3:11 NASB 1977*

What John said Jesus would do is to send fire to the earth and put fire in the hearts of men. This symbol portrays power. Fire has the power to warm you and keep you alive, or destroy you. Fire purifies. Heat purifies the food we eat and the water we drink. Fire can symbolize suffering, anger, destruction, purification, or strong conviction. We see in whatever context, it always portrays something very powerful.

The fire of God, which is the anointing, develops strong beliefs or opinions as the Spirit of God reveals the Word of God, as supernatural encounter takes place. It is the anointing that people see, so we must firmly establish the quality that brings God glory and satisfaction. This is walking with God in the anointing's power. The fire of the anointing seeks to remove all that pollutes one's life. It is the process of extracting everything that belongs to this world so that the believer would be spiritually or ceremonially clean for service. The anointing will bring a consciousness of evil so that the believer would engage in purification. We normally do this through repentance, inner healing, and deliverance.

Scripture reveals that there are three baptisms for the believer. The baptism of water, the Holy Spirit, and fire. The Scriptures also show that "baptism" in Biblical Greek means "immersion," and the New Testament precedent set was that of baptism after conversion. Many times, the Holy Spirit manifests His power in the baptismal tank, revealing His witness and work in the believer. It is a powerful thing to watch most who are baptized receive the baptism of the Holy Spirit with the evidence of speaking in tongues. To watch the Holy Spirit deliver the one being baptized of demons or to watch them shake coming up out of the waters. It is important that the one who is doing the baptism be anointed themselves and the new believer be totally immersed.

These three baptisms correspond to the three sections of the Jewish Temple. We enter the outer court through water baptism, then the inner court through Holy Spirit baptism, and finally the Holy of Holies by the baptism of fire, to be in the presence's fullness of God.

As we walk with God in the anointing's power, just as the temple entrances in the tabernacle became progressively narrow, our walk with God narrows and the anointing's power becomes stronger as we get closer to Him. In each phase, carnality is being stripped away to reveal the Spirit of God within. The fire of the Almighty is consuming our selfishness, self-consciousness, and even self-control, because He wants full Lordship. In the Holy of Holies, the only "self" left is the "heavenly Man." The "old man," the man of flesh, has been burned away (1 Cor. 15:45-49) because he cannot enter the kingdom of God (v. 50). The fire of God through earthly tribulations bring transformation; It is a supernatural fire and cannot be so easily categorized. Once the anointing comes, we describe it as immediately the [Holy] Spirit forced Jesus out into the wilderness.

Therefore, the anointing seeks full immersion so we can burn brightly within us as lamps to give light to others. He also fills us with another kind of fire - a supernatural boldness and power to proclaim the kingdom, to intercede for all people, to pull down spiritual strongholds of wickedness, and to do many great exploits to bring glory to God's name. When I speak of full immersion, God takes action of immersing that believer into the anointing. It is that hot oil of heaven that envelopes us for action. We have our children go to these schools that immerse them through a method of teaching a foreign language by exclusive use of that language. This is the anointing! We exclusively use it for God's glory, His satisfaction, His excellence, His Kingdom to come to earth, His eternal purposes, His attention to detail, His mercy and severity, and how God classifies things. When we walk with God, the design of the anointing wants to manifest, but it is in the way we think on how powerful the anointing will manifest.

People ask us why have fire services. I simply tell them through proper choices that the fire of God's anointing will bring the believer closer to the Father. It has the ability to cleanse if the believer will allow. God's fire desires to bring a boldness and a power to the believer if they choose to step out in faith. The fire of the anointing will deliver someone of evil or heal a person's body. The anointing of fire is to bring the things of the Kingdom of God and put them into action. Therefore, the anointing can do all things, but will the believer allow that to happen?

The Day of Pentecost was a baptism both of the Holy Spirit and of fire. There was a rushing mighty wind, and there were tongues of fire. This is in direct relation to the pillar of cloud and fire that led the Israelites through the wilderness. The cloud and fire were two parts of the same pillar. This pillar was a witness, a guide, and a protector. God was dwelling in this pillar. We see this in every service, the cloud or God's presence, the fire or the active work of the anointing. The Apostles immediately became bold and preached Jesus.

For us personally, the Lord dwells in a pillar of cloud and fire within the hearts of the believer. We who have been baptized in the Holy Spirit (the cloud), we also should expect to receive the fire of God. The cloud and the fire are even now being poured into those who are hungry, and in fact, some are corporately becoming a pillar of cloud and fire. This cloud and fire are a single unit, like the Spirit, same word as "Wind" in Hebrew and Greek, and the fire of God is dwelling within us.

The fire of the anointing brings the power of darkness to their knees. The deliverance anointing has such power that even the fallen angels in the second heaven can't stand against the believer who has allowed the Holy Spirit to train them. There was fire by night, so the anointing brings those things that can't be seen out into the open. As I have pursued the anointing on my life, God has always been faithful to bring more of His Kingdom to light and also has been unfolding the secrets to the kingdom of darkness. The cloud by day is to transform everything that can be seen. It brings vision, awareness, confidence because it is the anointing that has brought those things out into the day. Peter says we are the children of the day, not of the night. The anointing causes us to walk in the light and empowers us to see where we must go. Jesus immediately knew that He was to confront the powers of darkness in the wilderness. It is the anointing that gives the drive and desire to confront demonization, sickness, and sin. The cloud by day or the anointing shields us from our enemies and the things of this world.

Before closing this chapter, I would like to make one more powerful point that every believer must understand and come to grips with. The Holy Spirit came down from heaven and Jesus received the full measure of the anointing. That anointing lead Him to a desert and to a forty-day trail of fire through temptation and suffering. Moses spent forty years in the wilderness learning its ways. It is only through this revelation that God uses a believer in this setting to lead God's people and rescue them from Egypt or the powers of darkness. Those who do not understand the kingdom of darkness can only bring a measure of help and freedom. The wilderness became an object lesson in the anointing's power and trusting God through difficult circumstances. We know as well it was a test of Israel's obedience. When we walk with God through the anointing's power trials and hardship will come, but so will fortitude, perseverance, and faith win out. When the Israelites complained and rebelled against God, they were forced to wander in the wilderness for forty years until that entire generation of adults had died (Num. 14:32–33). Until we are ready for the next season in our lives and a greater empowerment of the anointing, we will remain in that time of learning and growing in God, being strengthened.

Chapter Nine

Faith and the Anointing

There is a theme central to the Bible's total revelation, and that theme is faith. Who can fully measure or express the possibilities represented by that short word known as faith? Perhaps the best way to see what is possible with faith is to look at two scriptures Jesus spoke:

> *With God all things are possible. (Matthew 19:26)*

> *All things are possible to him who believes. (Mark 9:23)*

Jesus says within each of these scriptures, "all things are possible." We quickly notice that God can do all things, but Jesus extends the possibilities to the believer who believes. It is easy to accept that all things are possible with God, but can we equally accept the fact that all things are possible with the one who believes. Jesus points out that through faith, it makes the things that are possible to God equally possible to the one who believes.

As the believer takes steps of faith and believes God for the things promised in the Bible, the anointing moves. It is the yielded heart that believes and through surrender the anointing moves in power. Faith comes from the heart and a life surrendered to God; This is the anointing's power. The believer who operates in the anointing grows so much faster in faith than the one who does not. The one who operates in the anointing knows that God is with them and desires to reveal and strengthen the one who has faith.

The anointing demands surrender and to walk with God in an increasing expression of dependance on God. There is the gift, but the gift without the anointing brings no power, because the gift requires no faith. The gift will bring the presence, but the gift and the anointing brings power as faith operates.

Since faith is in the nature, presence and promises of God, the believer must partner with the Word of God and the Spirit of God to bring those things of the Kingdom of God into reality. This is walking with God and bringing about what God desires.

We have two English words for faith: the noun, faith and the verb, believe. We should not distinguish between "believing" and "having faith," for there is no basis for this distinction in the original Greek of the New Testament. As far as the Bible is concerned, believing is exercising faith. Conversely, exercising faith is believing. When we are walking with God in faith, it activates the gifts of the Holy Spirit and it is the anointing's power that manifests.

> *Now faith is the assurance (title deed, confirmation) of things hoped for (divinely guaranteed), and the evidence of things not seen [the conviction of their reality—faith comprehends as fact what cannot be experienced by the physical senses]. Hebrews 11:1 AMP*

> *Now faith is the substance of things hoped for, the evidence of things not seen. Hebrews 11:1 NKJV*

Those who operate in the anointing cannot help but grow in faith as the result of being continually exposed to His nature through His Word and His manifest power. Since this is so, we must understand what faith is. First let us look at substance! It is that which provides the basis for trust and reliance. The root definition is a legal or official document to effect a transfer. We could say that it is a written agreement. Substance literally means "that which stands under or provides the basis for." We comprehend that faith provides the basis for every legal and official scripture that the Bible offers in Christ Jesus. Therefore, faith is real; faith is a substance, and it is the anointing of the Holy Spirit that transfers those written legal and official promises of God.

Second, faith is evidence or the adequate proof of the truth. The root definition is the evidence that makes someone fully agree, understand, and realize the truth of the validity of something. This definition says we base it on an argument or discussion. I think it is better that we say, based on a discussion or promise that is legally binding officially. This is what the anointing is for, to take the legal promises of God and impart them to the Church and the world. Two verses below we see that faith is directly connected to the invisible.

> *By faith we understand that the worlds*
> *were prepared by the word of God, so that*
> *what is seen was not made out of things*
> *which are visible. Hebrews 11:3 NASB*

The scripture states that there is a contrast between the things that are seen and the things that are not seen between the visible and the invisible. Through faith, we travel behind the visible to the invisible—to the underlying reality by which the Kingdom of God operates and the reality of the Word of God. This reality is the basis for the operation of the anointing. When the believer walks with God according to the scriptures, the anointing stays activated and can be switched on immediately as we act on God's Word.

Therefore, faith relates to two eternal, invisible realities: to God Himself and to His Word. We walk with God through intimacy, surrendering each day to His Word so it does not hinder the anointing. We must live a surrendered life to the Holy Spirit, believing that through the anointing God will be glorified in who we are and all that He does through us. It is a powerful thing to walk with God.

It is not the presence of the Lord that positions us for miracles, but the understanding of how God does things. I have seen Baptist who have not been baptized in the Holy Spirit operating in the power of God. Why? Because the believer understands how God's Kingdom operates. The one who does not have the baptism of the Holy Spirit is greatly hindered, but operates out of the realm of faith based on God's truth. Just as the one who operates out of the baptism of the Holy Spirit and not the anointing, that person too is hindered. It is the anointing that activates the atmosphere. From the realm of the anointing, the believer speaks and realities manifest.

The believer who positions themselves in the presence walks in fellowship with God. He is the one who desires to agree with God. That believer will not rob God of His tithe, but will offer more than their money, a life laid down. To watch greed in the body of Christ is an indication that the believer wants God on their own terms. Therefore, God is limited to how He can use them. The believer who does not believe that the tithe is relevant in the New Testament Church says, God, you are not the same yesterday, today, or forever!

God's presence is an invitation to know Him and to walk with Him, but it is the anointing that ushers us into the impossible. As I have said earlier in this book, the anointing will invade realms not known to a man so that believer can bring a breakthrough for God's people. The anointing is never to be used to gain wealth, but to provide a lifestyle that is comfortable. The anointing is for the nations!

When God is with us, it will always require something. The anointing is the Lord's divine calling upon one's life. The anointing also possesses a deeper significance, including that of being singled out by God for special favor and responsibilities. The anointing is a summoning or an authoritative call to appear before God for a legal matter. God anoints so the believer can carry out legal matters for the Kingdom of God. He also gives the believer a measure of faith to begin the journey in the anointing.

When Jesus was casting out demons in Mark 1, the demon said, "What business do You have with us, Jesus of Nazareth?" The anointing is doing Kingdom business. A business is a person's regular occupation, profession, or trade. It is an activity that someone is engaged in. God calls and anoints the believer to walk with God and to do Kingdom business for God by saving souls, healing the sick, and casting out demons. The anointing dwelling in the believer says, this is the work that has to be done and matters that have to be attended to. We could say, it is the practice of making one's living by engaging in the anointing. The centurion understood his responsibility and carrying out his assignment.

As Jesus went into Capernaum, a centurion came up to Him, begging Him [for help], and saying,

*"Lord, my servant is lying at home paralyzed,
with intense and terrible, tormenting pain." Jesus
said to him, "I will come and heal him." But the
centurion replied to Him, "Lord, I am not worthy to have You come under my roof, but only say
the word, and my servant will be healed. For I
also am a man subject to authority [of a higher
rank], with soldiers subject to me; and I say to one,
'Go!' and he goes, and to another, 'Come!' and he
comes, and to my slave, 'Do this!' and he does it."
When Jesus heard this, He was amazed and said
to those who were following Him, "I tell you truth-
fully, I have not found such great faith [as this]
with anyone in Israel. Matthew 8:5-10 AMP*

Faith is a powerful reality that exercises government. This is great faith, walking with God and exercising His governmental rule. The centurion had Romes backing to enforce the law. When we realize that God created us to enforce His laws, the anointing will elevate or promote the believer. We come to a place in our lives and ministries that is pleasing to God, and by faith release the anointing that transforms atmospheres like Jesus did with the centurions slave. The anointing only needs the believer to speak, because when a believer speaks from the anointing's authority it releases the power to accomplish what he or she spoke. Jesus makes a powerful statement at the close of our scriptures, "I have not found such great faith as this with anyone in Israel." Great faith speaks with the knowledge of the Kingdom and how Kingdom business operates. Once the words are released in the atmosphere, the measure that the believer operates in that authority comes with power.

WE WALK BY FAITH

Let us look at our next scripture and conclude, if we walk by sight, we do not need faith. If we walk by faith, we do not need sight. The anointing will only operate out of the latter. There is a place in the spirit realm that our mind must go; that place is where the voice of God operates. I can look right at a cripple person but not really see them. I know they are crippled but I focus my mind on the anointing and a word from God that could change everything.

For we walk by faith, not by sight.
2 Corinthians 5:17 NKJV

We must first believe before we can see. This principle is so valuable to the operation of the anointing. Believing cause us to act in faith and see the authority of the anointing. In Psalm 27:13, David said, "I would have despaired unless I had believed that I would see the goodness of the Lord in the land of the living." What was true for David is true for all of us, he believed first? What kept David from depression was that he believed in God. If we focus on our circumstances, the power of God cannot do its work. Most of the things we go through in this life is for our eternal life. God knows what is in man, and He refuses to leave us in our fallen condition.

Jesus said, "Remove the stone." Martha, the
sister of the deceased, said to Him, "Lord,

by this time there will be a stench, for he has been dead four days." Jesus said to her, "Did I not say to you, if you believe, you will see the glory of God?" John 11:39–40 NASB

Faith empowers us to see the unseen and thus equips us to endure when the visible world offers us no hope or encouragement. The most powerful point in this scripture passage is, "Did I not say to you." Martha was about to get a lesson on the authority of the anointing by Jesus who walked with God. Jesus places a demand on all who desire to see the glory of God. We must believe that we will see. We do not see first, then believe. We believe first: then, because of believing in the anointing's authority, we see the power of the Holy Spirit. When we walk with God, He will show us things to come. I like that, it could be immediate or future, but it is coming.

Regardless of our level of faith, God will also have a miracle waiting to advance one's faith. To walk with God, we need to know Him and encounter Him through the anointing. The student of the anointing is always looking for the nature of God. Jesus addressed Martha's issue of faith by exposing her unbelief and then encouraging her to believe.

I understand when some say that Jesus never withheld a miracle because of faith in a small measure. However, sometimes the miracle does not happen. Jesus could meet every condition because He had the authority and power to forgive sin. One thing I've learned in over 20 years concerning miracles, we must meet the condition. God is merciful, but He is also just. Again, Jesus healed everyone who came to Him, regardless of the person's heart condition, that is God's desire. We each realize that walking with God we must agree with God. That our hearts are transformed daily. Jesus' heart was and is perfect in every way and He had and has authority to forgive sin. There are some that the mercy of God releases healing, but most healing and deliverances happen when the conditions are met.

Some people address the little faith issue in Matthew 17:20, and comment on unbelief, humiliation, and condemnation, or say it was to position the person to grow in faith. This all sounds reasonable, but the disciples had run into a spiritual realm they lacked training for; their training to that point had not equipped them. The Biblical definition for littleness in Matthew 17 is to not have enough faith or to have limited faith. It means a state of having little or inadequate faith. The disciples put what faith they had into action by attempting to cast out according to the knowledge they operated in. We all do this every day. To say that their unsuccessful attempt was due to unbelief or to position them to grow in faith is just not so. When we act in accordance to our faith and are unsuccessful, there is a good possibility that the faith exercised was not enough because of lack of experience. To have a limited amount of faith is to exercise under limitations of the anointing due to inabilities or lack of talents. Inadequate faith restricts the operations of the anointing because the believer lacks adequate knowledge of the realm they are seeking to operate in. When the Lord spoke audibly to me and said, "You must respect your enemy and be fully trained," I was trying to cast out a demon I lack supernatural knowledge to take authority and exercise power. This is walking with God in the anointing's power!

Here is the basic conflict between the old nature and the new nature. The old nature demands to see, since the old nature lives by the senses. God has to deliver us from that old nature and that old way of life and bring us to a new nature and a new way of life.

> *For momentary, light affliction is producing for us an eternal weight of glory far beyond all comparison, while we look not at the things which are seen, but at the things which are not seen; for the things which are seen are temporal, but the things which are not seen are eternal. 2 Corinthians 4:17-18 NASB*

There is great importance in the word "while": "while we look not at the things which are seen." It points to the same lesson Moses learned in his test of endurance. He learned that, in the sovereignty of God, affliction serves a useful purpose for believers. It forms and strengthens our character and prepares us for the eternal glory that lies ahead. But the lesson that the word "while" teaches us is this: Affliction serves us only while we keep our eyes on the invisible realm. If we lose sight by becoming preoccupied with the world or its time and of our senses, we can no longer receive the benefits that affliction should provide for us.

So we are caught between two worlds: the temporal and the eternal. The temporal is what we can see; we contact it with our senses. But the eternal is the world God wants us to be at home in. And we can be at home in that world by only one means: faith. Faith is the one thing that connects us to the unseen realities of God and His Word.

When we walk with God in the anointing's power, there will be trials that this life demands character and the mental and moral focus to see the unseen. There comes a time in each one's life we are to live through the spiritual sense and not the physical senses. As stated before, the lesson that the word "while" teaches us is this: Affliction serves us only while we keep our eyes on the invisible realm. This is so powerful in developing our anointing. Standing in faith for years if need serves as a measure for the things to come.

Therefore, the anointing empowers faith and lifts us above the realm of our own abilities and makes God's possibilities available to us. The anointing driven by faith connects us to two unseen realities: God and His Word. As we walk with God in relationship through faith, it enables us to endure and to overcome the tests and the hardships that confront us in our daily lives. These trials become opportunities for God to reveal to us and others His goodness and His glory.

There is an ongoing struggle between faith and sight. Our old nature is at home in the world of the senses, and it demands us to see. As believers, we need to cultivate the new nature through the power of the anointing, which trusts God and His Word without demanding other evidence.

Before closing this chapter, I would like us to look at the word "producing." It means to cause a state to be and God is doing it for us. What state is that, affliction! The definition tells us that God is preparing us or working in us like a farm that tills up his field to plant for the next season's harvest. God's desire for our eternal glory is so intense that the definition points to Him doing it thoroughly and successfully. It means to do something with success and thoroughness. Yes, the anointing will perform signs and wonders, but it also goes deep into the heart to prepare the believer for the age to come. When the definition speaks of causing change, it could point to a total overturning. The anointing will completely overturn our previous life and begin to impart a totally different life. The anointing causes transformation!

Therefore the anointing produces service which is the main or end result. The one who says I am anointed but does not serve does not operate out of the anointing. It goes totally against Biblical definition. Anyone who says he has encountered the Lord, but is not willing to serve, we should question their self motivation.

CHAPTER TEN

THE ANOINTING WORKS THROUGH FAITH

How can we be sure that the words we use in our admissions really proceed from genuine faith in our hearts? Scripture gives a simple, practical answer to this question: Faith that is confessed with the mouth must be backed up by appropriate actions.

For just as the body without the spirit is dead, so also faith without works is dead. James 2:26 NASB

Most believers focus on the second part of this verse, but I would like to comment on the first section of the verse. The body without the spirit is dead, that is the formula to raising the dead. We are asking God to return the human spirit to the body along with the soul. As the anointing moves on the believer, it is vital that our words through prayer line up with scripture. I have seen this personally! I was doing a deliverance on a young man, when a demon of death came up and said, "I am death and I own him," at that time he fell dead. The Holy Spirit had me pray Romans 8:2, "For the law of the Spirit of life in Christ Jesus has set you free from the law of sin and of death." Immediately, the young man came back to life. It was the Holy Spirit's leading to pray that scripture, and it was the anointing that brought him back to life. You may ask, how long was he without breath, about five minutes.

Once faith has come, there are three phases of development through which it must pass: confession, outworking, and testing. The growth of the anointing is dependent on how the believer responds to these phases. I am informing the reader, if you will go through the process and develop calling things that be not as if they are; working or acting on the scriptures; passing God's timetable; all things will be possible.

The words confess and confession are important scriptural terms with a special meaning. The Greek verb homologeo, normally translated "to confess," means literally "to say the same as." Some Bible translators use the related words profess and profession in place of confess and confession. Regardless of which word is used, the basic meaning of confess and profess remains the same: "to say the same as." Therefore, we directly relate confession to God's Word. Let us look a little deeper into confession. The word "confess" is homologeō (ὁμολογεω), made up of homos (ὁμος), "same," and legō (λεγω), "to speak," thus, "to speak the same thing," thus, "to agree with some person with reference to something." Therefore we are to be in agreement with scripture.

Amos said, "How can two walk together unless they agree?" Walking with God and in the anointing's power, we must speak or confess the scriptures. We must say the same things God is saying! If I don't confess or speak, then faith will not grow. We sometimes call this declaration. I confess something like, "I decree and declare," and then I speak scripture. That is how that young man came back to life. I had to agree with God.

A similar thing happened a few years ago. There was a man dying because of infection. The doctor could not stop whatever infection he had. The wife came to one of my meetings and asked me to go to the hospital and pray for him; I did. As the Holy Spirit spoke, I spoke, and his body began to shake. The shaking brought about consciousness. As I continued to confess what the Holy Spirit was saying, his right eye opened, then his left. Minutes later he began talking and one week later he was released from the hospital. What happened? I came into an agreement with God and the power of the anointing saved his life. Words of knowledge are powerful and gives the anointing opportunity to move. Confession is saying the same with our mouths as God says in His Word. It is making the words of our mouths agree with the written Word of God.

In Psalm 116:10, the psalmist said, "I believed, therefore have I spoken". In 2 Corinthians 4:13, Paul applied these words to the confession of our faith: "But having the same spirit of faith, according to what is written, 'I believed, therefore I spoke,' we also believe, therefore also we speak." Therefore, the natural way that faith is demonstrated is through speaking. When we speak, the power of the anointing looks to touch all who believe.

The Bible makes a connection between our hearts and our mouths. Matthew 12:34 says, "You brood of vipers, how can you, being evil, speak what is good? For the mouth speaks out of that which fills the heart." Going back to the end of the last chapter, the old man speaks from what is morally wrong. Jesus asks them, how can you speak what is good when you yourselves are evil? It directly links the power of God to speaking. We probably do more damage to ourselves than the devil does by the way we speak. This will hinder the anointing.

If we fill our hearts with faith, then that will be expressed in what we say with our mouths. But if words of doubt or unbelief come out of our mouths, they inevitably show that there is doubt or unbelief somewhere in our hearts. We can offer our own opinion on the condition of our faith, but God does the final inspection. No-one can bridle their tongue, but the Holy Spirit can control it if we allow Him to.

CHAPTER TEN

FAITH SPEAKS

Paul shows us how one comes to salvation in Christ Jesus. He also lays equal emphasis on faith in the heart and confession with the mouth:

> *But what does it say? "The word is near you, in your mouth and in your heart"—that is, the word of faith which we are preaching, that if you confess with your mouth Jesus as Lord, and believe in your heart that God raised Him from the dead, you will be saved; for with the heart a person believes, resulting in righteousness, and with the mouth he confesses, resulting in salvation. Romans 10:8-10 NASB*

In each of these verses, Paul speaks about the mouth and the heart. There is a three-step process we cannot overlook. We begin by confessing God's Word, then we start to receive it into our hearts. Then faith comes and we need not consciously attempt to confess because it comes naturally. We know that walking with God is to agree with what He is doing and saying.

I confirmed the way this process works to me one day when I discovered that the phrase for "to learn by heart" in the Hebrew language is "to learn by mouth." I saw that the English phrase "to learn by heart" describes a thing to be achieved. The Hebrew phrase "to learn by mouth" describes the practical way in which we achieve that result. To learn things by heart, we repeat them with our mouths. We continue saying them over and over until doing so no longer requires any effort. In this way, what begins in our mouths eventually becomes permanently imprinted on our hearts.

The heart is the central or innermost part of us and where our thoughts and emotions pour out. As I search the scriptures and confess them, my heart changes and faith arises, then the anointing flows. When our hearts are enjoying what God has called us to, faith acts, and the anointing comes forth. Faith is one of the central keys in the New Testament. The more our faith makes progress, the deeper the revelation we have of God's righteousness, His ways, power and the anointing.

Doctrine is something people like to live by and try to explain through works. When the anointing comes, truth is what we become, and it transforms us into the image of Christ. Truth stirs the heart of faith and causes that believer to act, putting our faith into works or action. The anointing will lead us into the experiences of what Jesus has accomplished. Once we have become accustom to confession, then we start to walk. We understand that walking is a moderate pace, and it gives us the opportunity for reflection. The anointing can never be rushed, but as we lift and set down each foot in turn faith grows and the anointing flows.

When the New Testament is speaking metaphorically about walking, it means to follow a certain course of life or to conduct oneself in a certain way. This brings the power of the anointing. When our conduct and the fruits of our lives look more and more like Jesus, the power of the anointing flows.

Throughout the New Testament, the verb "walk" is qualified in various ways to ensure that the reader understands what correct Christian living or conduct is and what it is not. Believers are not to continue to walk in darkness (1 John 1:6; 2:11). What John means is that believers should not continue living in ignorance of divine truth, an ignorance that is associated with sin and its evil results. Along with this, their walk should not be characterized by craftiness and cunning (2 Cor. 4:2) or by such sins as immorality, impurity, passion, evil desire, greed, and sins, the writer says, which are used to characterize their continual living before salvation (Col. 3:5–7).

May we always remember that we do not obtain freedom by our feelings but by the Spirit of the Lord; the one and only thing that makes us free is the truth of God empowered by the anointing. The believer should not be deceived but should always remember that the anointing operates from a matter of truth, not a matter of feelings. Feelings can cause us not to speak in faith, but say things that are negative, and destroy the work of the anointing.

Did your parents make you recite the multiplication tables? My parents sure did. Even decades later, I still remember my time tables. In the same way, we can have the Word of God permanently imprinted on our hearts. Again because this is so important; Our feelings may prompt us to say something that does not agree with God's Word. But we must persistently resist our feelings and make the words of our mouths agree with God's Word.

JESUS AND THE ANOINTING

The Holy Spirit was the sole source of Jesus' ministry and He is that same source of power for us today.

> *how God anointed Jesus of Nazareth with the Holy Spirit and power, and how he went around doing good and healing all who were under the power of the devil, because God was with him. Acts 10:38 NIV*

In this one verse, we identify all three persons of the Godhead. God the Father anointed Jesus His Son with the Holy Spirit. The result of the total God in action on the level of humanity was healing: "he went around doing good and healing all who were under the power of the devil." The anointing of the Holy Spirit was the secret and the source of the ministry of Jesus. Jesus went around doing good and healing all who were under the power of the devil through the anointing. When speaking of the devil, scripture refers to both all the fallen angels and demons.

> *In my former book, Theophilus, I wrote about all that Jesus began to do and to teach until the day he was taken up to heaven, after giving instructions through the Holy Spirit to the apostles he had chosen. Acts 1:1-2 NIV*

CHAPTER TEN

After Jesus' resurrection, He was still completely dependent on the Holy Spirit and the anointing. Jesus gave prophetic instructions through the gifts of the Holy Spirit. We also depend on the Holy Spirit and His anointing. We know that this happened during the forty days after Jesus' resurrection and ascension. Our challenge today is to depend on the Holy Spirit as much as Jesus did. The anointing is the power of the Holy Spirit who raised Jesus from the dead.

Jesus also promised that His disciples would receive the same Holy Spirit that empowered and influenced Him.

> On the last and greatest day of the festival, Jesus stood and said in a loud voice, "Let anyone who is thirsty come to me and drink. Whoever believes in me, as Scripture has said, rivers of living water will flow from within them." By this he meant the Spirit, whom those who believed in him were later to receive. Up to that time the Spirit had not been given, since Jesus had not yet been glorified. John 7:37-39 NIV

Through the indwelling Holy Spirit and the anointing's power, Jesus has become the supply source of every believer who seeks to operate in the anointing. The invitation is to anyone thirsty to come and drink. These scriptures reveal two things, one the baptism of the Holy Spirit and two, the outpouring of the anointing. Therefore, all who come and receive would do likewise becoming a source for those people coming to that believer. Jesus said streams of living water, this means multiple anointing that bring life to dead places in people's lives.

Jesus through the anointing awakens each believers true identity. The Holy Spirit touched me, but when the anointing came, I operated out of power for service. When we are empowered by the Presence of God through the anointing, the Holy Spirit awakens your true potential, positioning you to step out in works of service and be the person you were divinely designed to be.

The Holy Spirit lives within you and everything He has called you to be and everything His Word describes you as—this is who you really are. However, it is the anointing that will bring it to pass. I see many believers baptized in the Holy Spirit but not living out their destiny. As the Holy Spirit drove Jesus to the desert, the anointing defeated the devil, and the anointing will drive us to destiny. It is the anointing that changes the believer into another person. This happened to Peter as he continued to operate in the anointing. Peter went from leading a prayer meeting to his shadow producing miracles.

The apostles performed many signs and wonders among the people. And all the believers used to meet together in Solomon's Colonnade. No one else dared join them, even though they were highly regarded by the people. Nevertheless, more and more men and women believed in the Lord and were added to their number. As a result, people brought the sick into the streets and laid them on beds and

> *mats so that at least Peter's shadow might fall on*
> *some of them as he passed by. Crowds gathered*
> *also from the towns around Jerusalem, bringing*
> *their sick and those tormented by impure spirits,*
> *and all of them were healed. Acts 5:12-16 NIV*

I understand what people are trying to say when they write about Peter's shadow releasing the presence of God. However, this is not scripturally correct. The presence of the Holy Spirit is His person, but the anointing is His power. The presence dwells in and upon, but as Jesus said in John 7, it is the anointing that flows out like rivers. To live from the indwelling Holy Spirit is the power of the anointing. It is that dwelling in and upon that produces a dimension that changes atmospheres. As that river flows out of the believer, it changes the surroundings and their conditions. The anointing powerfully touched all who laid in Peter's jurisdiction.

In my early days, I could feel the Holy Spirit in me and upon me, but when I laid hands on someone, all they could feel was a little spark. Nothing coming out of me to change anything. However, I continued to dwell in the presence of God and read His Word and things slowly began to change. I would see some healed and some freed of demons. As I learned to grow in the anointing, more and more supernatural activity started to take place. This is walking with God in the anointing's power. I needed to learn how God did things and to agree with Him, then I had to change.

I really love this passage of scripture! Through the power of the Holy Spirit, God added to the Church. Why did people come? God was saving, healing, and delivering people. I'm sure there has been a lot written about Peter's shadow. I will attempt to give a very basic imagery. We find the imagery of the shadow in the book of Hebrews. Hebrews tells us that Jesus is not only the great high priest but the sacrifice as well in 9:6-14. In the Old Testament, ceremonial sacrifices and practices were only external regulations, applying until the time of Christ. The Bible emphasizes the imagery of animal blood in Hebrews as a shadow of the effectual cleansing of the blood of Christ. My take on the shadow was a supernatural manifestation of the power of atonement. Peter walked in such a revelation of the power of redemption that the supernatural was manifested.

We see power ministry following those whom the Apostles raised up when they preached Christ crucified. Peter's sphere of authority was the presence on him and the anointing coming out of him. He was walking in relationship or agreement with God and the anointing's power was touching and exercising control over an environment. Let the reader understand, there is a difference between living with the Spirit dwelling within and upon us verses walking in the anointing's empowerment.

The people brought the sick into the streets and laid them on beds and mats so the anointing could heal the person who was suffering from an illness. There was more going on here than just healing. The Strongs definition says the weak, infirm, and feeble were touched by a shade caused by the interception of light. God's presence or the light that Peter walked in and the anointing or the action of preventing someone or something from continuing in the same state touched the sick. The people were laid on beds and mats, indicating they were suffering from an illness and in distress. Who were these people, my Bible Logos program says they were invalids, lunatics, paralytics, people with skin diseases? Not only was there healing, but there was deliverance too!

Peter walked in such agreement with God that God's presence and anointing released supernatural healing and deliverance. Let me give my version which I don't normally do. The Bible states that the apostles performed many signs and wonders among the people, and it added more and more men and women who believed in the Lord. Could it be that those who were saved through signs and wonders laid their sick and loved ones in the street because the Church was so busy. Could it be that those who were touched by the work of the Holy Spirit brought those they knew to Church. People seek and become increasingly aware of God's presence and His power in different churches. God has called the Church to represent Jesus accurately in both word and the work of the Holy Spirit. We can't do this unless the Church walks in unity with God, transforming into the image of Christ and allowing the Holy Spirit to work. It is time for the body of Christ to open our eyes and see the wondrous reality of becoming one with Christ. It's the anointing's power that will change the world.

In closing this chapter, faith takes its stand with the facts of God's Word and confesses them as true. Feelings may waver, but ultimately, if faith stands fast, feelings will come into alignment with the facts. Walking with God and in the anointing's power, we must speak or confess the scriptures. We must say the same things God is saying! The Bible makes a connection between our hearts and our mouths. God desires us to walk more in the supernatural ministry by agreeing with Him. After Jesus' resurrection, He was still completely dependent on the Holy Spirit and the anointing. Dependence is what the anointing will form inside the believer. Walking in the anointing is the action or power the Holy Spirit seeks to transform lives. Peter walked in such agreement with God that God's presence and anointing released supernatural healing and deliverance.

Chapter Eleven

The Power of the Anointing

There are four powerful truths listed in Acts 2:42: instruction of the Apostles, fellowship, eating together, and praying together. Instruction from the Word of God is powerful. We get saved because we believe in what is being presented. One must believe in their heart that Jesus is the Christ and confess with their mouth. Therefore, we are saved because we believe in Jesus, but we will have a supernatural influence and sphere of authority and power because we believe like Jesus. Jesus never moved the Kingdom of God forward by good conduct or how He felt, but by what He believed. It is the same today what we believe and the instruction we receive is what we are today. What we believe and the level of instruction we receive directly impacts the anointing's power.

There is one thing I have learned in over twenty years of ministry, people's actions and choices will impact the quality of their lives, how they respond to Church leaders, and if they will ever choose to step into the anointing. It is vital for the believer to understand that choices, leaders and the anointing are key to upgrading one's quality of life and conduct. If we can have good beliefs in what the Word of God says, good beliefs about our leaders, and good beliefs about others, then it reveals that the believer has good beliefs about themselves. If someone does not like someone, it reveals that they, in some degree, don't like themselves.

The question is, do you love your neighbor as you love yourself? The Holy Spirit will expose a believer who desires to be like Christ through how we feel about ourselves and this is to some measure how we feel about others. Do we truly love God's people or just some of them?

Those who become great leaders believe in the people they lead. The question is, who is truly following that leader? Except for the young, rich ruler, Jesus invited those to follow Him. Leaders are always on the lookout to see who has a desire to follow them. People who have leaders in their lives generally rise to the level of the anointing that God has for them.

Jesus revealed a principle that every leader today must focus on: that is, to be an empowering influence we must have empowering beliefs. If I am to empower those who follow me, I must have that reality living inside of me. I cannot give what I do not have. The believer who does not spend their whole life in supernatural ministry, that is, prophesy, healing, and deliverance, cannot properly lead people. This is not my statement, but based on the life of Jesus.

> *And as you go, preach, saying, 'The kingdom of heaven is at hand.' Heal the sick, raise the dead, cleanse the lepers, cast out demons. Freely you have received, freely give. Matthew 10:7-8 AMP*

This reality may be hard to swallow if your deliverance ministry does not match your healing ministry then that believer is not an adequate leader. Jesus' ministry was well balanced. Those that operate in powerful healing realms usually only graduate to the realms of sozo deliverance. If one is moving in miracle healing, that person should also move in exorcism.

The anointing will always bring us into new realms of thinking through scriptural revelation manifested in power. We see many who desire to follow leaders who move in power, so later it might dominate our future. We should ask ourselves, is a leader doing the same thing for the last ten years; that leader has lost the desire for more of God.

There are Church leaders today that say, many believers emphasize a lifestyle of "spiritual warfare" to combat the ploys of the devil, but it is important to understand that the highest level of spiritual warfare is to take "every thought into captivity." Do these leaders actually listen to themselves? To take every thought into captivity is a sign we need deliverance. These leaders also leave out verse 6 in the 2 Corinthians 10:4-5, not understanding that verse 6 is the power verse. Here's my point: a good leader will teach from experience not out of opinion or personal belief.

Have you heard some says that those who think the second Corinthians passage is talking about pulling down strongholds of the devil, but it is actually referring to addressing our own belief systems. We would not need inner healing or deliverance if we could address our own strongholds. We could hear the truth and it would set us free. A good leader will address falsity!

THE TRANSFERRED ANOINTING

As a good Father, God is looking for people who are willing and pliable. Leaders are looking for those who will accept the call so they can transfer the anointing. The anointing is transferred by anointing with oil, but that is only the beginning. God cannot put new wine in old bottles. This is what I mean about being pliable. If I don't change, the anointing will leave. I cannot get God to do what I want; I must learn what He wants and do it.

The believer seeking the anointing must make sure their life is fit for service. I don't seek the anointing so I can see God heal; I seek the anointing to bring glory and pleasure to God.

God's continual presence is for our fellowship with Him, yet He gives the anointing so we can serve Him.

CHAPTER ELEVEN

We begin to know God through His presence, while His anointing is given that others might know Him through us. The anointing is power, and it is for service, not fellowship. We enjoy fellowship through God's presence. When God's presence comes, I ask Him, is this for fellowship or do I move into service so that the anointing flows?

Most do not know how to go from the presence of God into the anointing and the acts of God. The presence will not activate the gifts, but it is the anointing that operates out of the gifts. God's presence strengthens my human spirit, but the anointing will affect the human body. In most cases, God always requires a person for the anointing. God can do all things, but the anointing is for service. If we only do what we love, the anointing will never come near your house.

God's presence brings us into fellowship with Him. That is what this book is all about. Fellowship means we are to agree with God and walk with Him. The presence brings us into an ever deeper and increasing intimacy with Him. We start to feel God's desires and seek to know Him better. From the presence comes the voice of God, we learn to hear Him. We feel those unctions or impressions; those knowings in the heart; We hear His thoughts and at times we hear His audible voice.

The anointing will lead us to places in the supernatural that bring revelation to our hearts and requires Biblical study. The anointing cannot flow unless we are walking in fellowship with God. It also requires us to live in fellowship with others.

God requires the believer to keep the anointing. If we are prayerless, distracted, lacking in discernment, involved in sin, too focused on ministry, not exercising our gifts, the anointing will leave. The anointing lifts us into supernatural dimensions.

As Christians, we believe that we will function in a totally different way in the next age. We will be set free from many of the limitations of our physical bodies, because God will give us a different kind of body and a totally different lifestyle. But many Christians do not realize that, through the Holy Spirit, we can taste a little of this lifestyle right now in this life. We can taste "the powers of the coming age." We can only taste them, not appropriate them in their fullness; but we can come to know a little of what the next life will be like even during this life. Therefore, through the Holy Spirit and the anointing's power we can have a taste of the age to come.

God is holy, so He requires those who walk with Him to live holy lives. As the believer operates in the anointing that one will see holiness manifest as God moves. I spend a lot of my time in ministry cast out demons, understanding what brought demons, and what God requires through casting out. Let us examine several scriptures from Leviticus, because the theme of the book of Leviticus is holiness—the word "holy" occurs there over ninety times.

For I am the Lord your God. You shall therefore

consecrate yourselves [consecrate means "to "sanc-tify" or "to make holy"], and you shall be holy; for I am holy. Neither shall you defile yourselves with any creeping thing that creeps on the earth. For I am the Lord who brings you up out of the land of Egypt, to be your God. You shall therefore be holy, for I am holy. Leviticus 11:44–45 NKJV

Speak to all the congregation of the children of Israel, and say to them: "You shall be holy, for I the Lord your God am holy." Leviticus 19:2 NKJV

Consecrate [sanctify] yourselves there-fore, and be holy, for I am the Lord your God. Leviticus 20:7 NKJV

And you shall be holy to Me, for I the Lord am holy, and have separated you from the peoples, that you should be Mine. Leviticus 20: 26 NKJV

By the clear suggestion of the scriptures, the require-ment for being God's people is to be holy as He is holy. This quality is what distinguishes and separates us from all other people on the earth. That you may distinguish be-tween holy and unholy, and between unclean and clean. One of the main themes of Leviticus's book is how to dis-tinguish between what is holy and what is unholy, between what is clean and what is unclean. In fact, one of the main responsibilities of the priesthood under the law of Moses was to teach God's people the difference between holy and unholy. The failure of the priesthood to do so was one of the main causes of spiritual and national disaster in Israel.

This same principle applies to Christian ministry. One of the great responsibilities of the ministers of God's people is to teach the true nature of holiness, including how to distinguish between what is holy and what is unholy. Where this teaching is not given, or is not received, spiritual disaster will always follow.

We find so many men and women who have been anointed fall from grace because of not practicing or living holy before God. If there is not a continuing presence of God in our life, we need to stop and repent for living unholy. God's presence is a design to always be with us; holiness is that attraction for the Holy Spirit. Right, Holy Spirit and the believer being holy!

One key to the anointing and the understanding of holiness is the practice of fasting. It has dropped almost entirely out of the picture, and the church cannot have a complete conception of the holiness of God without it. Connected to this missing piece is the loss of travailing intercession leading up to fasting. God only anoints those who walk in the Spirit, those who are crucifying the flesh and its deeds. Prayer, intercession, and fasting are keys to bring us into direct contact with our desires and the cravings of the flesh.

How we live under the anointing will determine the lasting fruit of our life and ministry. How we allow the anointing to manifest will determine how many lives it changes.

To those who have not pursued deliverance unto exorcism on a continual basis, many people will remain in bondage. Only anointed ministries have God's blessing and can expect to have a prosperous future. The success of every ministry depends on the anointing and how they allow it to touch people. Not every big ministry who operates in healing the majority of the time will have God's full blessing in heaven. Ministries who do not allow the anointing will be dead and lifeless. The Christian who is looking for a church home must understand what Jesus commanded the disciples in Matthew 10, preach the gospel, heal the sick, and cast out demons. This is the ministry the blessing of the Lord will be on, small or big.

The kingdom of God is a spiritual kingdom run by spiritual principles and spiritual power: "For the kingdom of God is not in word, but in power" (1 Corinthians 4:20). To be God's people, we have to be different—different in terms of holiness, separated out from all other people; we are to be distinct, unlike anything else, separate. Where there is no power, there is no holiness.

In Deuteronomy 14, we find almost the same wording as in the Exodus passage. The book of Deuteronomy is essentially an analysis of the conditions for entering your God-given inheritance and staying in it. And, like Leviticus, Deuteronomy puts great emphasis on holiness: For you are a holy people to the Lord your God, and the Lord has chosen you to be a ["peculiar"] people for Himself, a special treasure above all the peoples who are on the face of the earth (Deuteronomy 14:2). It is holiness that distinguishes them from all other people.

Paul speaks of the resurrection of the new man in Christ Jesus and makes a connection of dying to oneself and living for God. Holiness is the way to the anointing and operating in its power; it is impossible to be anointed if you are in the flesh.

In Isaiah 61 the scriptures states, the Spirit is "upon," not "with" or "in." The anointing is given for us to walk in covenant relationship, not living for ourselves but living for service and to see the following manifestations Isaiah talks about.

Here are the power functions of the anointing listed in Isaiah: It brings good news to the afflicted; bind up the brokenhearted; proclaim liberty to the captives; proclaim freedom to prisoners; proclaim the favorable year of the Lord; proclaim the day of vengeance; comforts all who mourns; gives beauty for ashes; gives the oil of joy; gives a garment of praise; cause former captives to become trees of righteousness; glorifies the Lord; rebuilds shattered lives; bring restoration and prosperity. The anointing is a powerful thing that God has given to the body of Christ.

The anointing brings numerous blessings, according to Psalm 89:19-29: This passage teaches that the following results will be seen upon those who are anointed: they will be called servant; God's hand will be with them; God's strength will be with them; they will know freedom from deception; they will know freedom from the affliction of the wicked; they will know God's victory over enemies; they will know God's faithfulness and mercy; they will have influence over nations; they will have a Father/child relationship; they will know God's saving power; they will partake of God's covenant; their descendants will be established.

The anointing brings physical healing, as Mark 6:13 teaches us: "And they cast out many devils, and anointed with oil many that were sick, and healed them." The anointing breaks bondages and relieves burdens, as we see in Isaiah 10:27: "And it shall come to pass in that day, that his burden shall be taken away from off thy shoulder, and his yoke from off thy neck, and the yoke shall be destroyed because of the anointing."

In Deuteronomy 26:18-19, the Lord has declared us to be His holy people. We are His valuable treasure or His personal wealth. It is a possession that is highly valued by its owner. The definition of a treasured possession, i.e., valued personal property, what is owned by someone, which the owner has a special affection or holds a special value. Not only are we anointed, but we are greatly valued by the Lord. Holiness substantially increases the anointing and brings people to the Lord. The definition does not put a value on the treasure meaning we can increase in value. The more we are conformed to the image of Christ, the more valuable we are to God for His service. A life laid down!

WIND OF THE HOLY SPIRIT

"...And the Spirit of God was hovering over the face of the waters." (Gen. 1:2) The Hebrew word for "hovering" here is "rakhaf," showing a brooding, as of a bird about to hatch an egg. This is a "birth," caused by the Spirit. There is to be new heavens and a new earth (Isa. 65:17, Rev. 21:1), and these are also given birth by the Holy Spirit. This process has already begun. The crown of this creation, the New Man, has already been conceived and is being formed, also by the same Spirit, and the same Breath of Life. God has sent His Spirit and anointed this new creation to bring about His administration. It is a powerful revelation that God is brooding over us to bring about the fullness of the new man. The anointing has come to aid in this process. Man was created to walk with God in fellowship and intimacy, but we were also created to agree and rule.

The word "wind" in Hebrew is "ruakh," and in Greek is "pneuma" (whence "pneumatic"). Both of these words also mean "spirit" (or "Spirit"). In an English translation of the Bible, we see "ruakh" or "pneuma" as "wind," "spirit" or "Spirit," depending on the translator's decision on how to render it. The original text often contains double or multiple meanings.

"And suddenly there came a sound from heaven, as of a rushing mighty wind, and it filled the whole house where they were sitting." (Acts 2:2)

On the Day of Pentecost, this mighty rushing wind was

also a mighty rushing Spirit. The very nature of the original text was intended to provoke thought, and looking at both meanings of the word will enrich us. When we think of the word "spirit" (or "Spirit") we think of an unseen person or being. The Father, Son and Holy Spirit are persons. Yet there is something in the connotation of the words, "ruakh" and "pneuma" which is missed in English, as it depersonalizes nouns. The Holy Spirit, as seen in the original texts, is a living Wind - or living Breath. Let us look at Jesus' conversation with Nicodemus, paying attention to the original Greek translation, to bring out the duality of the words in question:

"That which is born of the flesh is flesh, and that which is born of the Spirit (Wind/Breath) is spirit. Do not marvel that I said to you, 'you must be born again (or: born from above.).' The wind (spirit/breath) blows where it (He) wishes, and you hear the sound of it (Him), but cannot tell where it (He) comes from and where it (He) goes. So is everyone who is born of the Spirit (Wind/Breath)." (Jn. 3:6-8)

Jesus was describing the nature of the Holy Spirit. He is invisible. He moves, although He is also still (1 Ki. 19:11,12). No one understands where He is going or where He came from. He is a great mystery. No one can control Him. When he moves mightily, He affects the physical world. Like a hurricane or tornado, He can destroy when He moves in power. He also moves gently, like a refreshing breeze in the heat of summer.

In Jn. 20:22, Jesus breathed on the disciples, saying, "receive the Holy Spirit" (pneuma hagion = Holy Spirit/Wind/Breath). This was very significant. God breathed into Adam the "breath of life, and man became a living being." (Gen. 2:7). When Jesus breathed on the disciples, He introduced a higher sense of the breath of God - the life of the Spirit. The supernatural breath of God has the power to bring our spirits to life, and this same breath also has power to quicken (bring life to) our mortal bodies (Rom. 8:11).

On that day of Pentecost, suddenly a sound came from heaven like a rushing violent wind, and it filled the whole house where they were sitting. The fire of the anointing moved the Apostles from a prayer meeting into their destiny and the construction of the Church. I say construction because they together went through a learning process. The anointing is the tool God uses to change a world and to change a person. To walk with God is to live a life of mysteries that come with an invitation to discover where the Kingdom of God is going. The walk of faith is to live a life of revelations entrusted to us with the purpose of sharing them with the world.

I hope you have enjoyed the book as much as I have in writing the book. It is my heart to see more of the body of Christ touched with the anointing and to move in the power of the Holy Spirit. I have left the book with a closing bang, leaving room for part two. May God richly touch your life and may you walk with God in agreement as the anointing reveals the priceless treasures of God's Kingdom.

Hungry For More Information?

Conferences

More information
churchinoneaccord.org

REFERENCES

Amplified Bible (AMP)

Copyright © 2015 by The Lockman Foundation, La Habra, CA 90631

The Holy Bible, New King James Version

Copyright © 1982 by Thomas Nelson, Inc. Nelson, Thomas. Holy Bible, New King James Version (NKJV) . Thomas Nelson. Kindle Edition.

New American Standard Bible-NASB 1995 (Includes Translators' Notes)

Copyright © 1960, 1962, 1963, 1968, 1971, 1972, 1973, 1975, 1977, 1995 by The Lockman Foundation

A Corporation Not for Profit, La Habra, California

All Rights Reserved

The Lockman Foundation. New American Standard Bible-NASB 1995 (Includes Translators' Notes) (Kindle Locations 1410-1412). The Lockman Foundation. Kindle Edition.

Logos Bible Software 7 - Copyright 1992-2018 Faithlife/Logos Bible Software.

© 1998 by InterVarsity Christian Fellowship/ USA ® All rights reserved. No part of this publication may be reproduced, stored in a retrieval system or transmitted in any form or by any means, electronic, mechanical, photocopying, recording or otherwise, without the prior permission of InterVarsity Press.

Leland Ryken, James C. Wilhoit, Tremper Longman III. Dictionary of Biblical Imagery (p. 1058). InterVarsity Press. Kindle Edition.

EXPLORING SECRETS
OF THE
HEAVENLY REALMS

VOL. 1

AVAILABLE ON NOW AMAZON

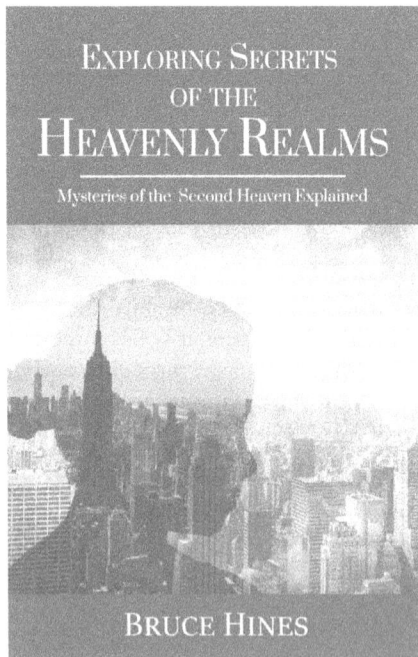

EXPLORING SECRETS
OF THE
HEAVENLY REALMS

VOL. 2

AVAILABLE ON AMAZON

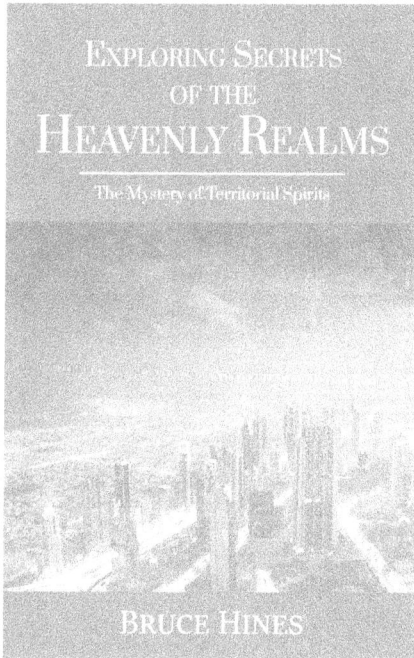

EXPLORING SECRETS
OF THE
HEAVENLY REALMS

VOL. 3

AVAILABLE ON AMAZON

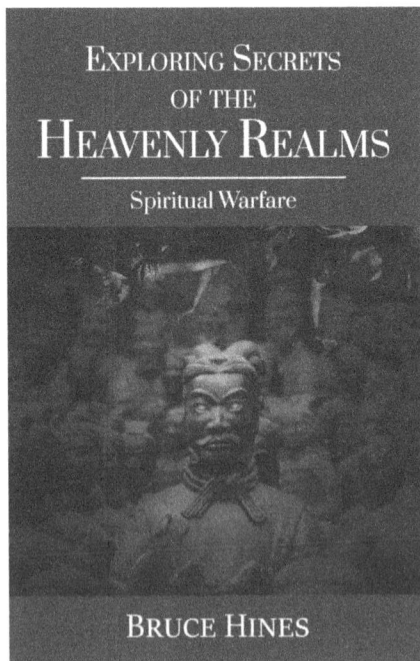

EXPLORING SECRETS
OF THE
HEAVENLY REALMS
Spiritual Warfare

BRUCE HINES

EXPLORING SECRETS OF THE HEAVENLY REALMS

VOL. 4

AVAILABLE ON AMAZON

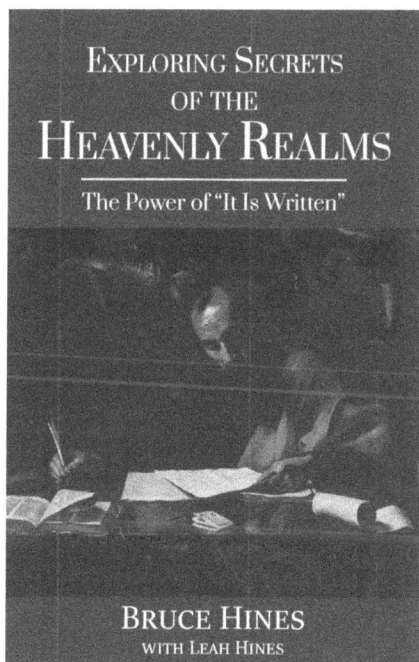

EXPLORING SECRETS
OF THE
HEAVENLY REALMS

The Power of "It Is Written"

BRUCE HINES
WITH LEAH HINES

EXPLORING SECRETS
OF THE
HEAVENLY REALMS

VOL. 5

AVAILABLE ON AMAZON

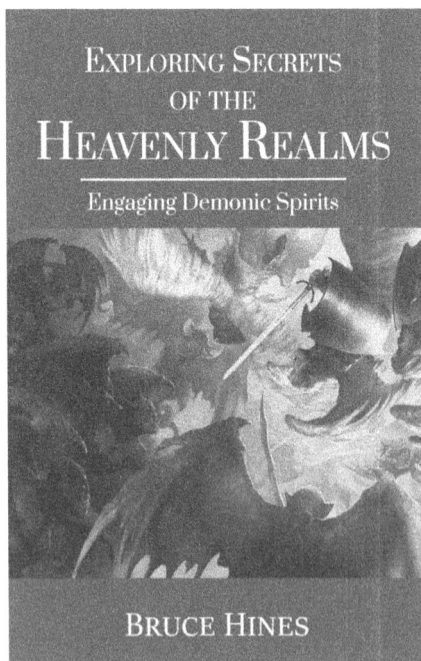

EXPLORING SECRETS
OF THE
HEAVENLY REALMS
Engaging Demonic Spirits

BRUCE HINES

THE MYSTERIOUS KEY
TO THE
NEW TESTAMENT

AVAILABLE ON AMAZON

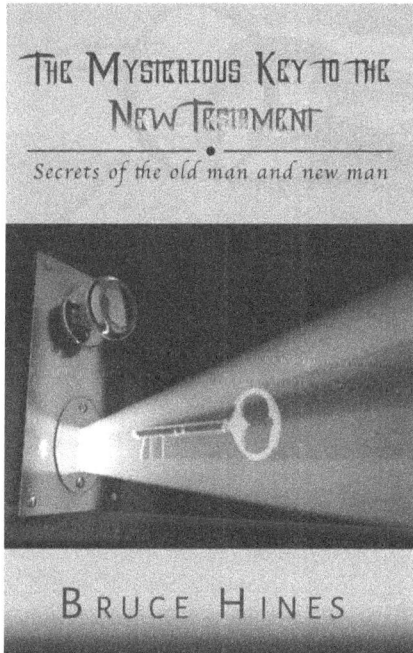

www.ingramcontent.com/pod-product-compliance
Lightning Source LLC
Chambersburg PA
CBHW072140090426
42739CB00013B/3239